Healing Humanity

ISBN: 1-4392-4954-7
ISBN-13: 9781439249543
Library of Congress Control Number: 2009907034

To order additional copies, please contact us.
BookSurge
www.booksurge.com
1-866-308-6235
orders@booksurge.com

Healing Humanity

Life Without Shame

Anne Stirling Hastings Ph. D

2009

Table of Contents

Foreword

Anne has a remarkable way of letting the reader in on her journey of "Following My Feet," as she calls her intuitive unfolding of life. When I read her introduction it brought me to tears. She touched a profound knowing and understanding of the human condition. My condition. Me. Through her writing, her feelings, observations and story-telling, she is able to express a deep comprehension of how shame limits our gifts, our lovability, our joy, and our ability to commune with each other. I have read many self-help books and this one is really different. Anne has a willingness and ability to be transparent—and commune with the reader. We need people like Anne all around us.

I grew up crippled by debilitating toxic shame, that hideously painful feeling. As one of Anne's co-healers I have eliminated so much of it that when Anne asked if I would write a foreword, my immediate response was excitement! But then came fear and the bubbling up of old feelings of being not worthy—shame, of course. However, having the skills of shame-healing, I knew that this was an opportunity to diminish more shame! And I did right then and there. I felt lighter, now with the freedom to be excited over telling you about Anne and *Healing Humanity*.

This book is different, offering a full opportunity not only to see how your life is being limited by shame but how it is possible to begin healing just by reading it! This is not because of Anne's intellectual understanding—which she has—but because of the loving energy she directs toward you that comes across even from the page. The book itself is shame reducing!

When you have finished reading I believe that you will feel authentically hopeful. You will see that it is possible to heal shame and have the freedom to love and commune with the world. I am grateful to be walking this journey with Anne, and I am excited that you are taking the steps to free yourself from shame and walk with her as well.

Elizabeth Wedington, Counselor
Tacoma, Washington
Author of: If He Would Just... Healing From Shame to Love

Introduction

I learned how to heal shame—along with the accompanying traumas and deprivation—as a psychologist seeing clients, and by doing it myself. Readers of my books repeatedly tell me that personal stories are useful, so I have included my own and others' to show how shame becomes attached to each of us, and how to remove it.

I have spent most of my life healing. My picture memory and emotional memory and body memory indicate severe emotional, sexual and physical abuse when I was very young. I was chronically depressed throughout childhood and early adult life, with occasional pleasant life experiences. Even before I was born my mother believed I had unusual powers, and she needed to make sure I used them for good instead of evil. She gave up, however, and viewed me as some strange alien, an identity I adopted. I developed what Attachment Theory calls Avoidant Attachment, which is self-explanatory. I was isolated and separate from the family and community. I never felt as if I fit in and belonged. Listeners have said I tell the experiences of my young life as if no one else had been there. That was how it felt.

Shame and fear and depression prevented me from using my intelligence, and from being curious about what was being taught. I created a life in fantasy that took up all my time. I did poorly in school, barely got into college, and didn't begin excelling until the middle of my sophomore year. In a college life away from home I made lots of friends, and for the first time, had a community. I began to enjoy school, discovering what I liked, and got a bachelor's and a master's degree in psychology. I earned my Ph. D. later.

When my son was born I fell into an intense, agitated depression. Years later I learned how giving birth brought up abuses from childhood, and fear for my son. I went into therapy, which taught me how one's history causes symptoms, and how we project childhood relationships onto the present, believing they are still true. I cried and talked for years in psychoanalysis, which helped, but back in the '70s trauma healing wasn't understood, and addiction recovery was new. Self-help books had not yet made it to the market.

When my son was five I returned to graduate school for a doctorate, and learned a lot more about myself, too. I studied Attachment Theory and came to appreciate the role of the child's early bond with the mother. It was many years until I understood that shame emerges from early lack of attachment. This helped me understand that while I avoidantly attached, and refused to believe my mother's view of me as evil, still I became heavily shame-based just from my unacceptability to her. My defenses against this emotional abuse were strong but unable to entirely shield me from her deeply held conviction of my horribleness. While other children develop active lives to offset their shame, I fell into depression. I felt as if I didn't have a life. When I was old enough to discover fantasy I imagined the life that I could have when I grew up. That was my best defense. But it was only a coping tool. It didn't change my internalized shame.

While Avoidant Attachment made me separate from others, feeling as if I didn't belong even when doing well in social circumstances, it had certain advantages. I have been able to think for myself, learn what I needed in order to heal, and create a career that was unusual for a woman then. I felt so outside the social norm that operating out of it wasn't threatening and didn't change anything. Even though my parents valued education, they reacted no differently to my poor grades in high school than they did to my getting a doctorate and beginning a practice. I was an enigmatic alien. They didn't know what to make of me.

Embracing a freedom that most people don't have allowed me to develop a practice that I call Following My Feet. This phrase arrived when I discovered the pleasure of going where my feet went on exercise walks with no plan about where, or how fast, or how long or how far. I had already come to respect that I lived according to my intuitive understanding of what was needed next. Being an alien, I didn't have to consider what was expected of me in this culture or by my family. Anything I did was no surprise. I did have arguments in my head about my decisions, however. But I never obeyed them. The arguments said things like, "Boy, is that stupid, you can't take time off to write, what about your expenses? This doesn't make any sense at all, you should be doing the logical thing." They tried to shame me and scare me.

Foot Following sounds like such a good thing, and actually it is, but it didn't become a source of safety and correctness as I imagine having a mentor—a real person—would. Instead, I was alone. But Feet keep me pressed against the next difficult task or emotional healing. Looking back on where my Feet have taken me is pleasurable, as I get to observe what I have done. But during the process, it is more like having to move forward whether I want to or not.

My emotional healing began when my son was born, as I said, and has occurred in bouts since. My life goes along seemingly normal for a while, and then some piece of traumatic memory leaps up for attention. Long ago I didn't understand why bad dreams, feeling horrible on awakening, or finding myself disoriented and spacey for most of a day was actually the experience of something that happened long ago. Now I understand, and so I set out to process each new piece. When sexuality was the focus of what needed to be healed I wrote books explaining to myself what sex was really about, and healing my personal and cultural abuses. The name of the first, *Reclaiming Healthy Sexual Energy*, was what I wanted for myself. The last, *Treating Sexual Shame*, wasn't fun to write because I had completed the education I sought.

I have yearned for friendships in which everyone would tell each other the full truth, once we could figure out what that was. We would take responsibility for our own experiences, and examine how they were projections from childhood trauma and deprivation, and work on healing them. As various people attempted to join me, it became clear how difficult this is. It brings on the very shame that we want to avoid. Yet, it also offers the opportunity to heal that shame. Over the years I could increasingly see that shame was the underpinning of what needed to be healed as well as the obstacles to healing. Healing worked best when shame was examined.

My thinking and writing shifted to toxic shame, a pain of every therapy client. Each individual must confront this limiting emotion in order to heal, which is difficult because we live in a culture that has integrated shaming and shame relief.

I focused on integrity for a time, calling my psychotherapy practice Integrity Resources. I wasn't looking at the moral view of integrity, but rather what makes things work right, like motors that hum in contrast to making scratchy noises. What did I, and my clients, need to know in order to discover our own integrity? What needed to be seen? And then healed? What would we automatically change if we gave ourselves the chance, and had the willingness to face pain to do so?

The themes of love and support and connection and community ran through my life and my work. As people get better in therapy they are more capable of accepting themselves, and then of loving openly and with great satisfaction. I could see that there is no shortcut to love. "Falling in love" doesn't bring love, it brings sexual bonding and a sense of permanence, along with temporary approval and adoration. This brings shame to a halt—for a while. Deciding to love doesn't bring it about either.

> *I came to see that our particular defenses*
> *against pain, and our projections of*
> *past relationships onto present ones,*
> *inhibit the exchange of love.*

These have to be healed in order to have the natural human experience of loving and receiving love.

I want the real experience of energetic connection and true seeing of each other—*communing*. I discovered that many people are capable of some of this. And my Feet showed me the process I had to go through to access my own capability.

I saw how I had attempted to ameliorate shame as an approach to getting better, and how that really didn't help. The shame was still showing up in dreams and occasionally wanting to be dead. Some people seem to be able to sufficiently avoid their shame to enjoy their lives and not have the need to heal it. I am not one of them.

Even while I was trying to avoid shame, Feet led me on a long journey of studying people all around me so that I could understand the role of culture in harming us, and inhibiting healing. Initially, I criticized people who acted according to the culture. Then, as I was able to observe the rules and order, I became able to just objectively observe. I accepted that I wouldn't fit in or belong, and began to value that.

Hatred, revenge, racism, sexism, addiction, rape, child molestation, child abuse, cruelty, economic recession, parenting difficulties, lying, employment conflicts, marital problems, most mental illness, and absurd reasoning by banks and stock purchasers based on greed, are caused by shame. *They are all caused by our inherent natural humanness interrupted by shame followed by countless methods of avoiding shame, resulting in the blind harming of every one of us.* Shame is the underlying culprit that has to be healed in order for everything else to work well. World peace cannot be obtained by political changes. Only when each one of us takes on the task of finding our integrity, which means engaging in the painful healing of shame, will we obtain it.

Healing shame requires facing shame. I am grateful that I instinctively did this.

> *I am purifying myself of shame*
> *in order to become fully human.*

I have progressively given up culturally prescribed means of feeling connected. I used work and parenting and social drinking and relationships and projects and sports and countless small methods to avoid knowing how little connection people all around me have. Finally, as I gave up these defensive maneuvers, I have come to see that:

> *Not a single person is capable of continuous intimacy,*
> *with no need for defensive maneuvers.*

Discharging shame and fear brings massive experiences of love and contentment and intimacy. Any fears I had about not fitting in, and losing all my friends and relatives, and feeling alone and isolated, and preferring to be dead than live the kind of life I had, *were not founded in reality*! When I hear friends and clients express these fears, I smile, because I once had them! Instead of things being worse, I have become able to have the love that is available. I belong in the whole world even when intimacy isn't possible. I can embrace all the wonderful arenas of life that I have developed. And I don't yearn for someone or something to make things better. The result of healing has been entirely positive.

Those fears, however, have alerted me to one of the many reasons to heal with a *group* of people: Belonging to a healing sub-culture provides connection until we reach the place where we know we are never alone.

Feet finally let me put together all the arenas of my healing, and see the big picture. The moment that happened I organized this book in my head. It took five more months and bad initial drafts to welcome this understanding and truly appreciate the level of my own healing. I used to say that none of us had enough years left to heal everything. No more! Now I know that I will complete healing of childhood trauma and cultural trauma. I have the skills, and I know how to remove the obstacles!

I wrote these next paragraphs one day when I was free of shame and any influence of my childhood. I am moving rapidly toward living there all the time.

I have a view of the universe, of existence, that includes each of us and every animal, cell, and atom. This space is organized, functioning, fluidly working. People who have understood this have called it god, god meaning everything and all the functioning within it.

Each person, each animal, has its planning, its instincts. Somehow toxic shame got introduced by humans, and the evolution of every atom's place in the universe got distorted. Toxic shame left us with emotions that don't make sense and an inability to use emotions to know what to do.

The distortion comes when we are conceived into existence and are not given what we truly need. We can't take our place. We can't see what is natural and correct, we lose perception of our instincts. We can no longer automatically respond to the emotional signals, like birds always looking out for predators, and cats alerted by unfamiliar noises, and babies crying desperately when left with a sitter.

Used well, religion, self-help programs, psychotherapy, spiritual practices, or taking care of one's home, yard, and family could lead us back to the shame-free existence and our place in the natural order of things. Some creators of religion understand this, and try to help people find their way back. But leaders of a religion who haven't healed their shame pass it along with rules.

Each one of us is a tiny cog in the big picture. And because we *automatically belong in the picture based on being conceived*, we should be able to function the way we are intended. Since shame is the enemy, we all get to heal shame. In fact, we must, in order to return to the natural order.

I couldn't understand, or see, the big picture of existence until I healed my shame and the effects of having been deprived of essential mothering when I was conceived and born. Right now I have no empty spot within. I belong in the world no matter how distorted all those around me are.

I am here. I belong. I fit in. I have life. I am entirely integrated into the universe. I am full, complete, alive, connected.

My Pod of Co-Healers

As I claimed my own shame-free life, and worked with others as co-healers, four of us became a Pod of women healing shame together. We tell each other the whole truth about what we are thinking, feeling, and observing about each other, and anything else. We create boundaries as needed, and rejoice when we can all be together to relate in our shame-free, shaming-free way. We accept our remaining symptoms of abuse and attachment deprivation. We each get to see that we are accepted as we are for who we are. Each of us is supported in discovering our gifts and interests, and developing them.

The Pod is as close to anything I have experienced of true communing. All of us get everything we want and need with no sacrifice of the wants and needs of others. We remain startled and amazed by how we support each other and are entirely supported, with no cultural or personal shame motivating us to entirely heal shame! We are joined by our commitment.

We know how to heal shame. We know how to heal the attachment deprivation that contributed to shame. We know how to become clear of projections from childhood relationships, even while knowing we will still run them on each other.

Chapters 12 to 18 explore how to heal shame in the following ways:

- Join a group of people who are healing their shame. Being with others who are doing the same is infinitely more helpful than trying to do it by yourself or even meeting with a therapist individually.

- Learn to recognize shaming behavior. Study the culture to see how people shame each other all the time. This education is necessary in order to stop taking it in, and to stop agreeing that it is normal and appropriate. See how parents shame their children.

- Study your own experience of shame, noticing how it feels in your body—is it in your stomach, on your skin? Your face, your neck?

- Let yourself feel the emotion. Keep breathing so it can move instead of stagnate. Let it be discharged out of you. Grieve it away with anger and tears. It can eventually all bleed out.

- Learn the methods that you use to avoid feeling this horrible emotion. Do you become defensive and lash out? Do you cower, feel like a victim, rationalize, accuse others of doing what you did? Wear the right clothing, be polite, work hard, stay busy, be good? Do you try to fit in?

- As shame heals, it will bring healing from childhood shaming and traumas and deprivation of love, too. This brings freedom to discover what you are doing here, and your role within the huge community.

This book is about:
- acculturated toxic shame
- how it cuts us off from ourselves

- how we defend against feeling shame, with resulting social consequences
- probable culture without shame
- and how to heal all kinds

Chapter 1
Shame: The Basics

What Is Shame?

Most simply, shame is a terribly unpleasant emotion. Healthy shame is a gentle alert that tells us we would be happier if we shifted gears. Toxic shame, a term offered by John Bradshaw in his best seller, *Healing the Shame That Binds You* (1988), is that dreadful sense of badness. It can include feeling pointless and hopeless, deadened, with no reason to go on. It is the greatest enemy of living a rich, communal life.

Shame can be experienced in many ways, including anxiety, depression, loneliness, yearning for love and contact, wanting evidence of success, and fear of being seen. It can be a heaviness that separates one from other people, and from oneself. Apathy, lack of interest and lack of pleasure are signs that shame is dominating.

Bradshaw's book is known by most people engaged in serious addiction recovery. A revised, updated edition published in 2005 can be useful to read as well as other books that delineate shame. Staying immersed in the subject for hours helps counter the denial of its pervasive nature.

We All Have Toxic Shame

Every single one of us carries shame. We believe that we are bad or harmful or terribly flawed, and we try to figure out how to not be. If we can just be good enough, or polite, or helpful, or successful, or wealthy, or spiritual enough, then we can believe that we aren't bad after all.

Since shame inhibits us from really knowing who we are, we lose sight of the fact that we were all born full of love and life. We are forced to learn how to develop our loving selves because we have been presented with shaming and brainwashing that interfere with automatic access to our human potential. If we didn't believe we were shameful we wouldn't need to be told what being good and being bad are. We would just know. We wouldn't need to learn how to pray, or to forgive, because these are automatically within us. We have been harmed, and so we must heal. If we had not been harmed, we would have nothing to heal with spiritual and religious practice or by becoming "good."

The phrase, internalized shame, means that
shame has become part of one's very identity.

We believe it is who we are. My internalized shame came from my mother seeing me as unusually bad, more so than my innocent brother and sister. She communicated it with cold stares and a calm, hard voice. This made my heart stop, and I became ice cold in terror. If I believed my mother, as a child is wont to do, I would have felt so terrible that life would have seemed impossible to live. So I kept the shame outside of my soul by distancing myself from her, and then from everyone around me. Thus came the Avoidant Attachment style of relating.

Almost all children receive shaming looks and negative comments and impatience. The adverse impact of this would be less than when seen as evil because it is less shaming. The methods of defending against it would be smaller, too. My sister learned from me that if she were calm and good, our mother could be loving, and not very critical, so she integrated these behaviors into her view of who she was.

The overview of my childhood, and how I was shamed, is simple. It's more complicated to discover the details—what my mother said, what she did, her behaviors that year after year supported my understanding of her perception of me. One obvious example is her neglecting my need for braces by age twelve. Money was not an issue. My teeth were so bad that I never smiled with my mouth open.

It didn't occur to me to ask for braces when I was twelve because I was an alien. Only human children had this right. Internalized toxic shame included an identity of being not human. When my mother talked about how a neighbor's daughter worked to pay for her own braces, I didn't see myself as belonging in the same category.

As I write, it is startling to realize this truth. My parents were educated, my father a high status professional, we lived in a nice house, my mother stayed at home with the children, there were no divorces. These were the standards of respectability in my family. Yet inside that good presentation was the bizarre treatment of a child.

Healthy Shame

Bradshaw and others address what they call good shame in contrast to the toxic variety. Bradshaw sees shame as the motivator for humans to live good lives. I believe that we are born geared to have good lives. Integrity is natural and desirable when we get shame out of the way. It is a positive draw. Good shame and good guilt assist us when we shift away from the natural positive draw. It says, "Nope! Stop. Go the other way." When obeyed, integrity feels really good—not because it turns off a painful signal but because of having access again to the positive signal.

It appears that Bradshaw and other writers still see shame as an individual feeling, held within a single person; therefore, individual change is needed. However, I see healthy shame as having a community function along with leading us toward personal integrity.

We have lost most of our community orientation, and so all we can see is ourselves. The well working community described in *The Continuum Concept*, by Jean Liedloff, is fully supportive and integrated. Individuals don't sacrifice themselves or their uniqueness in order to belong to the larger group. Instead, people who haven't isolated their understanding of themselves and each other in order to hide from shame are able to be entirely themselves, meet their own needs and desires, and function fully in the service of the community. Being fully oneself and functioning fully in community aren't incompatible! This is how we are intended to live.

Feeling bad for harmful actions, such as lying, stealing, killing, etc., supports the existence of well-working order. Healthy shame and guilt are our signals that we are not doing our part. Somehow this shame took on far greater meaning and impact over history, resulting in a belief in one's badness instead of acting as a signal of having done something harmful and as a stimulus to right it.

Healthy shame and integrity pull us forward.
Toxic shame pushes us.

Toxic Shame

When I use the word shame I will be addressing toxic shame, the kind that makes us feel bad, not the healthy kind that alerts us to our deviation from functioning in a manner that supports healthy community. *Healthy shame is mild and feels really good!*

There seem to be *two kinds of toxic shame*. One is internal, our own voices received from countless reflections of badness. The other is the shame felt when seen by others if we are doing something defined as shameful by the culture. These include being bad, mean, unclothed, urinating or defecating, using bad table manners, being sexual and countless other acts.

The Shame System

Whenever two or more people join together to shame and counter-shame, or shame others together, or help each other avoid the feeling of shame, they are engaged in the shame system. This can take the form of one person shaming another, and the second shaming back—the circular argument. It can be seen when people join together to triangulate against or gossip about other people or institutions. It can be people rescuing each other from feeling shame, such as by joking about it. Our culture has complex rules about how shame systems work, which I will address throughout the book.

Toxic Shame in Everyday Life

Feeling like a bad, horrible, harmful person is perhaps the most obvious experience of shame. Other forms are reflected in our cultural descriptions, including low self-esteem, shyness, awkwardness, self-criticism, or a general feeling of hopelessness about life. Feeling unimportant to, or unloved by, spouses, friends, children and others is experienced as shame.

Fear of engendering feelings of shame prevents people from pursuing a life right for them, including looking for jobs, getting education or training, asking questions to find the right path, relating to possible love partners with ease and curiosity, and exploring satisfying places in which to live.

Fear of public speaking is fear of shame. If there are no true dangers awaiting, then fear is irrational. Some fear isn't of being shamed, but this is a good place to check when it shows up, because most fear is. Finding my heart rate increasing and my palms sweaty when standing on a cliff is from fear of heights. But the nervousness when giving a talk is from fear of feeling shame.

A woman explained in detail how it wasn't personal when she turned down my offer to play racquetball. She was trying to make sure I wouldn't feel shame at her refusal. She was avoiding feeling her own shame that would appear if she caused me to feel it. *Avoiding shame causes so much wasted relating*! We are compelled to learn how to avoid our own shame, and how to avoid "making" others feel it. Imagine how much energy and thought and creativity would be available to live life fully if we didn't have to attend to this emotion!

Asking for a raise, for a promotion, for time off, for a change in duties usually carries fear of disapproval. Disapproval isn't inherently harmful, but for those who depend on the perception of others to avoid feeling shame, disapproval can feel very harmful. The employer may feel uncomfortable saying no, and react with discomfort, perhaps wanting to shame the asking person to make it clear why he isn't qualified. The shame goes around and around, and the fear of being shamed does, too.

Being wrong in an argument, failing, letting people down, not seeing someone coming through the door, stepping on someone's foot, saying something objectionable: These are all experienced as worthy of shame—shame-worthy. So are burping, farting, smelling bad, or having stains on our clothes. When a champion athlete makes mistakes he is shamed by fans.

Being chosen last when team captains select players is told as a horrible childhood experience. All it means is that they thought you weren't good players. It has nothing to do with goodness or badness or the right to be alive. Failing in any way, including getting into college, getting degrees, getting jobs, getting dates, getting or accepting marriage proposals, and investing well have nothing to do with who we are as human beings worthy of life!

A boy in Starbucks about nine years old deliberately squeaked his shoes on his way to the bathroom. When he returned he asked his mother after they received their order if he could have some soy milk. She said no in a shaming tone. He obviously knew that he would receive that answer—that shaming.

Why do so many children do that? Some clients have explained that their childhood treatment was so bad, they actually felt better when they brought on abuse instead of waiting for it. Perhaps that was what the boy was doing. Or maybe his identity has become shame-based. Then it can actually be more comfortable to act shame-worthy to avoid feeling shame than to try to be good and still be shamed.

My mother criticized me with words like cold, hard, cruel, unkind, thoughtless, unloving, and selfish. She thought I was evil before I was born. I thought I didn't believe her, but I spent my life proving she was wrong, which is actually a kind of agreement that she was right. Occasionally I did things that I couldn't justify as not shame-worthy, and dropped into depression that included thinking that I had no life. Without understanding this, it was difficult to heal from my belief in my own shame. My conviction that all I had to do was prove I'm not bad set me up to continue feeling bad!

What about when a person does harmful things such as stealing, cheating, lying, manipulating, being unfaithful, hitting, abusing children, raping, or murdering? Healthy shame is an appropriate feeling because its purpose is to help the person stop the action *from the inside out* rather than from external controls. But intense toxic shame isn't helpful. In fact it is the reason people do these harmful things—*toxic shame has deprived them of healthy shame.*

Lying and Cheating

This subject deserves a separate heading as it is very common. I have been working with sex addicts and their spouses for many years, and have gotten to know what goes on in the minds of men and women who have sex outside of their relationship, and then have to create a network of lies to hide it.

If any of you have lived this way, you know that it feels miserable. First something drives a person to seek sexual intrigue outside the marriage, consisting of affairs, or just flirting or casual sex, or Internet porn, or computer or phone sex. The person who feels the need to resort to this way of becoming enlivened is almost always working hard to avoid feeling shame. But the way it is accomplished brings more shame. Then lying brings even more.

I have a client who came to me because he read an article I wrote called "Cats Don't Lie." He saw in my bio that I see sex addicts in my practice. He was filled with shame over his infidelities and lies to his wife. He was greatly relieved that I didn't add more shame onto the pile, and that I focused on removing it. Sadly, he had been shamed by his wife for twenty-five years and with her voice etched into his brain, he had a hard time believing me. He thought he deserved shaming.

He is healing his shame nicely, now. It is allowing him to step out of his brain—his intellectual defenses—and feel.

Popular opinion believes that men who cheat and lie are cold and hard, calloused against integrity. But the opposite is usually true. The attempt to stop feeling their high level of shame in turn brings more. Then the impaired relating with their wife and everyone else makes them feel removed and separate. Men who are able to begin healing their shame become available to experience intimacy. It is a pleasure to see a man who had lost that ability over his whole adult life be able to express it toward someone in his therapy group.

While it is obvious that the world has very many people who have no access to conscience, and others who commit crimes in order to belong, most lying and cheating are the result of toxic shame.

I have five cats, none of whom feels shame for anything. I love that. They also don't shame me! They may ask for what they want, even demand it, even getting angry when I don't provide it. But they don't think I am a bad person worthy of condemnation!

Our culture believes that anger is harmful because the object of the anger feels shame.

True anger is a natural emotion that can cleanse us of many kinds of distress. Anger typically expressed in a shaming, critical manner is something else. But even true anger is rarely well received. A vital component of grief, it functions to leave the past in the past so we can claim the present. It is an energizing, boundary-setting emotion. However, genuine anger has been maligned and is usually seen as harmful.

Gossip is the triangulating or joining of the good people against the bad or stupid or ugly ones. No one likes to be the subject of gossip. Why is that? It isn't pleasant, of course, but if we didn't carry our own internalized shame, we could simply know that these gossipers aren't communing friends, and let it go. We would have the freedom to merely see the truth.

"What are they going to think of me?" is a common expression of shame. "What will the neighbors think?" This kind of shame gets us to manipulate the neighbors' perception of us. In other words, deceive them. When we stop wearing the right clothes, buying the right car, smiling at the right times, we will indeed be the subject of gossip. Others will shame us. But they are shaming us anyway. No one is free from the shaming of others. We are too rich or too poor, dressed too well or not well enough. Something can always be found wrong with any one of us.

Again at Starbucks, I sat near a woman who seemed uncomfortable with my being there. I thought I might be too close for her comfort. After five minutes her friend arrived. She then asked me if she could remove her magazine from under my napkin, letting me guess that she had been trying to save the chair for her friend. I said I could move so her friend could sit there, and she thanked me profusely. Why couldn't she tell me she was saving the chair? Why did she need to thank me over and over? Why did moving have to be my idea? It was all shame—fear that I would provoke her internalized shame from the past. If she had been able to tell me, I would have said that there was no other chair available, but I would move when one was. We could have met both our needs—our real needs. Look at the stress she went through because shame prevented her from saying what she needed, and working with me to get it.

Shame is also called embarrassment, that feeling when someone comes to the door when you are in your bathrobe. Or when you don't hear what someone says and give the wrong answer. When the clerk is waiting for your credit card and you are waiting for it to be returned, not realizing you hadn't given it. When your children make too much noise in stores.

Getting Out of the "Shame System"

At a family visit I became aware of a shaming interaction, and by becoming aware, was able to step out of the shame system and not give an automatic response. During conversation, my son mentioned that someone had graduated from Service High School, which I had forgotten was the school he attended. When I asked where that was, he looked at me shamingly. His father, sitting next to him, gave me the same look. Their faces were contorted into the frown and mouth-clenching that communicates astonishment that a person could be so stupid-cruel-selfish-hurtful-thoughtless-unloving. My daughter-in-law scolded me, but in a humorous style that offered me a way out. I was to say, yeah, aren't I awful? And laugh with her.

However, because of the shame-healing I have done, I am different. In the past I would have said, "Well, what can I say!," and make some joke about being senile. By doing so, I would have entered the shame system. Instead, I said simply "It is a memory issue." The shaming from the men continued. I sat still and looked at them and really saw. I wanted to cry. I was being attacked—even while they would never think they were attacking.

I didn't feel shame. I never would have in this situation. But in the past I would have avoided seeing how I was being shamed by joining in the shame system. I could have said, "Well, I guess I'm just an idiot!," or challenged them with knowing the name of my high school, or stated that my brain is so full of important learning that I let the insignificant details slip out, or said what's the big deal about remembering the name of a high school. This would have been met with further comments, possibly referring to my lack of caring, or lack of intelligence, or it might have been done with just looks and sounds.

I used to use these maneuvers even though I didn't believe any of the criticism. By joining in the shame system, I wouldn't have even seen how their faces were so contorted into expressing hateful condemnation! I didn't see! And then I didn't have to react. But now that I was looking, and not responding in the system, I was able to see the degree to which harsh, mean, condemning treatment is doled out in the name of humor. I also see that they didn't know they were shaming me.

If shaming weren't integrated into the culture, these men would have reflected on my poor memory. They would have seen that I don't remember names well even though I am intelligent. They would have reminded me in a matter-of-fact tone that this was my son's high school. The way this was handled demonstrates how *there is no intimacy and compassion and caring and love and witnessing possible when playing in the shaming system.* And, need I even say this, there is no communing.

As I thought about my visit, I realized that seeing the shaming is more painful than responding in the system and not seeing it! Seeing and not taking on shaming sets me apart. I am really separate from these people. At the very same time, it allows me to heal from receiving shame, and from engaging in a false, harmful system. Apparently I had to be strong enough and far enough along in healing from being told I was evil, to be able to see clearly. I am strong enough to see the shaming, and to not take it on. It also requires strength to see how damaging these behaviors are to others, too, how everyone harms everyone all around them in an attempt to not feel shame-worthy.

Yet these very acts of shaming others
have to heap more shame on the shamer.

Even though I was astonished at seeing shaming directed at me, I appreciate being able to see the level of shame carried by others. Why would this family find it enlivening to humorously shame each other for hours at a time? They engage in competitive shaming, in a manner well within cultural norms.

When I was in my 30's and early 40's, I enjoyed shaming those who I thought deserved it. The president of a company pursuing my then-husband for employment was drunk and set out to establish that he could win a verbal encounter with me. I turned it back on him, putting him in the one-down position, getting the other execs and wives to laugh at him. I really enjoyed this. He set up the competition and I won.

Now I would find it satisfying to not engage. If he pursued, as he probably would after drinking all day at a ballgame, followed by a long period in the bar before dinner, I could have described what he was doing. Or I might have said nothing, just looked at him. My eyes and those of the others would have reflected himself back to him. I can still take charge, and feel personally powerful, but now in an entirely different manner. It might have saved him from being the butt of jokes at the office.

In order to not engage in his competition, I would have had to see what was going on. This is what has changed. My years of studying people in my office and in the world have educated me about the mental illness—which is really shame and the methods to avoid feeling it—that forces people to treat each other in mean ways. From this place of seeing, I can sidestep meanness.

People who cling to a victim stance use shaming others as a way to prevent feeling their own shame. A man explained to me how he had registered with the Do Not Call Registry, and when receiving a solicitation, asked for the name and number of the person. With great pleasure he informed her that he was going to report her. He received pleasure from getting one over on another, and again in the telling. I was invited to share my own examples.

A great deal of time and social interaction is spent telling stories that have to do with shame—shaming others, our own feeling of being shamed, winning over someone who is doing wrong, differentiating the good people and the bad people.

After I'd been talking about shame with a friend, she told me how her new awareness was helping. Someone called her mid-morning when she was still sleeping. Her friend said, "Shame on you for sleeping late!" Immediately she heard the word shame! We realized that her friend wasn't trying to shame her, she was responding out of cultural habit. My friend added that not only was this phrase coming from her friend, it was backed up by the whole culture! I imagined the Verizon ads with the man standing in front of a mass of people, offering a vast network of help. In this case, the vast network of shame!

Teasing children "playfully" can be shaming. At the beach, a little girl in bare feet asked her father in a whiny voice to carry her back to the car. He said playfully, "What, you want me to carry you? You're heavy!" She says, "I'm not heavy." He replies, "Yes, you are, you're a big girl," all in a playfully shaming tone. He seems to be a sweet father, but he is conveying that she is wrong to ask to be carried, that it is an imposition. Instead he could have explained that he isn't strong enough to carry her that far, and that she would have to walk.

Status

Acculturated shame conveys that status connected with jobs and wealth and education means that some people are worth more than others. They are higher on the ladder. Barack Obama's inaugural speech fluidly reached out to us as a community, preparing to work with us to undo the damage to our economy. But when newscasters spoke of him, they included the high level of his and Michele's education, supporting the belief that they are superior to the masses. Instead, we could all be glad for them that they found right ways to use their intelligence and interests, and that those ways support our needs for governing, our needs for community. It doesn't make them more worthy people.

Instead of lauding people who are wealthy or educated,
and by default putting down those who aren't,
a healthy culture would
support all people in discovering the right way for each to live,

for each to develop gifts and interests.

Then all of us could best support individuals and community. No job would be valued over any other job. Valuing would depend on the personality of each person, and what the job means to them.

Depression and Anxiety

Depression and anxiety are seen as mental symptoms and are addressed by therapy and/or pharmaceuticals. Therapists can help relieve these symptoms by changing beliefs that bring them on, or by assisting with grief for past traumas. Underlying depression, anxiety and panic is shame.

Many clients will understand that the sources of their feelings of self-hate need to be addressed. These include abuse—physical, emotional and sexual. They also include shame-filled marriages. Symptoms arise because methods used to diminish this shame aren't working well. *Healing internalized shame will heal depression and anxiety.*

I was seriously depressed in my early life, and it didn't abate until I had been in therapy for some time. Back in the '70's the primary benefit from talking and crying every week was being listened to, having my needs taken seriously, and feeling cared for. I saw this therapist as a third parent, as it was clear that much of what I received had not been available when I was growing up. This kind person who took me seriously gave me something that countered the beliefs I had developed from being raised by a hating mother. I had an emotional experience of the truth—my mother was wrong. I wasn't evil. I was capable of being a good mother and a loving person.

Since my depression came in part from negative feelings about myself, sitting across from someone who didn't agree with that assessment was quite powerful. The internalized shame from my mother's views was replaced by self-acceptance which became possible from having a valid reflection of who I am. My therapist saw me as loving, competent, intelligent, and with a right to be in the world. He didn't think I was an alien. While no one else thought I was, either, my style of relating with distance kept me from taking in this view. It took intense sessions for me to let down my guard and actually grasp that I was seen, and that what was seen was not an evil alien.

The depression lifted, I went to graduate school, and started discovering many ways to heal. As I learned to help others, I learned how to help myself, too.

How Shame Was Placed on Us

Head-shaking, eye-rolling, criticism, name-calling, saying "How could you have done that?" or "What were you thinking?" are some obvious examples. Impatient tones and annoyance are usually shaming. When my son was a young child, I spoke with impatience and annoyance when he did things against the rules. I asked my sister if she thought my approach to discipline was acceptable. This was so mildly abusive compared to how our mother had treated us that neither of us could see that it was shaming!

Less obvious examples of shaming are calling sex nasty or dirty, or telling children not to touch their genitals or anus. Even frowning in discomfort communicates that the observed behavior is shame-worthy.

Judgments based on race, religion, gender, occupation, education, income, life-style, sexual orientation, disability, intelligence, and mental illness, etc., are all examples of groups of people shaming other groups of people.

I spent a few days with an extended family. Since I was studying shaming I was tuned into all the examples. Everyone shamed the children, and all the adults shamed each other in many different ways. And the children shamed the adults. This last was punished, and the children were told in angry voices not to talk that way. The children also shamed and controlled each other in child versions of what the adults did.

This way of relating is seamlessly integrated into our society. A few years ago I would have felt discomfort, but not understood why. I have learned to recognize the small put-downs, and in particular, humorously delivered shame.

This family I visited is normal, friendly and sociable. They welcome their friends openly and create warm social events. The parents are truly dedicated, wanting to do the best they can. Not only are they normal, they are exceptional. Yet they continually operate on acculturated shame, passing it along.

Shaming is set up by evaluating a child's performance, even when the response to the behavior is positive. The child who reads more books than anyone in his class and studies things he is interested in is praised for being the best. Along with other forms of shaming, he is set up to think that his value is associated with what he does. Any time he fails to be the best, or even very good, he feels devastated. Shame.

The father of the one year old told him no, stop crying, stop reaching for the potatoes on the table. He gently slapped the boy's hand. This child is being taught that his normal, age-appropriate emotions and curiosity are bad. This translates directly to believing that he is bad because of course his emotions are who he is. Our emotions are who we are. He is being conditioned to stop using the emotions of grief, necessary to move from era to era of life. He is trained to not be curious. Curiosity is not allowed to be part of his identity.

*Since our emotions are who we are, if we are shame-based,
our identity includes the belief that we are bad.*

This father is working hard to control his son and turn him into a child that is easy to be around. This could be lauded. However, the father is so out of touch with understanding his son's appropriate emotions that he cannot know that what he is doing is harmful. It is clear that the father loves his son. He feels affection for him. He is responsible, makes sure he isn't harmed, eats on time, gets his nap. He is doing all he is capable of based on social norms and his own childhood.

Another time I watched a little boy excitedly tell his mother that he found a penny on the ground. She said in a shaming, aren't-you-stupid tone, "So you found a penny on the ground." If I told her she was shaming him, she might respond with how he finds so much on the ground and expects her to be excited about it when she has real problems to think about. She communicated to her son is that he is stupid or wrong to be excited about finding a penny, when in fact, it is totally natural and human for a boy of his age to be excited.

Our task in healing shame is first learning to see how it is going on all around us. Here is an example of shame that seems so small and subtle that most people would believe it couldn't possibly cause damage. Yet, this is the kind of treatment that clients remember when working on depression or anxiety. One man said, "My mother always acted like I was just too stupid for words. Even when I got accepted to college, she said I should have been accepted to a better one. She didn't come to my graduation. So now I don't tell her how successful I am and how much money I make because I know she will somehow put it down."

The mother of the boy with the penny was shaming in order to not feel her own shame. She has to make others' interests meaning-less.

Chapter 2
Early Shaming: Attachment Deprivation

Attachment deprivation in childhood
causes internalized shame.

We need to feel securely attached to our primary caregiver to feel safe and to believe that life is worth living.

When children form a secure attachment in their first year of life, they know they are loved. Someone knows what they need even when it is barely expressed, and meets that need with pleasure. Babies' instincts tell them this is right, and this gives them an appropriate experience of life—safe, secure, belonging, fitting in, having one's love received, being seen accurately, being understood. When the instinctive knowing of what is needed is satisfied, no shame is created. The child doesn't have to make up that something is wrong with him that has caused the mother to not do what is right.

The securely attached child will grow up with shame, too, but it is shaming that comes later, and is moderated by the good first experience.

Lisa's mother hid her pregnancy until she was in labor. Sylvia wasn't married and, with a career, the last thing she wanted was a baby. Even though she was very thin she had been able to bind herself sufficiently that little Lisa didn't show.

Sylvia called her mother on the way to the hospital, telling her for the first time that she was pregnant. Lisa was clearly not wanted. More than not wanted, Sylvia had tried to abort Lisa early in the pregnancy.

At her birth, Lisa was welcomed by medical people, but not by her mother. She was held with interest by her grandmother, and went to live with both women. The grandmother, retired and widowed, took over her care, as it provided her with something to do. Depression had prevented her from having much of a life. However, she lacked the ability to form a secure bond with a baby. While her care was superior to Sylvia's rejection, Lisa wasn't loved in the way babies need to be.

What did this do to her? The harm was actually great. We feel sorry for babies and little children who don't have loving mothers. Lack of love and an inaccurate perception of the child and her needs influence emotional development. They can create what is called Anxious Attachment, or Avoidant Attachment, two approaches the child uses to try to handle relating.

Lisa was seen as a bother or an inconvenience, and as company for an older woman. She did what we all would do—she believed that the attitudes toward her reflected who she really was. This means that on a deeply subconscious, non-verbal and elemental level she believed that she was an abuser of her mother and a pet to her grandmother. Since she wasn't seen as the loving, curious, life-filled person she really was, she had to believe that their attitudes were about who she actually was. She had no reflection of her real self. She was left with accepting the view presented to her: the reflection that she was harmful for even being alive, but had value in being a companion who didn't demand anything.

One might say, yes, yes, that's too bad, but she did grow up and get a better life, didn't she? Well, she did create a better life, but she carried with her the belief that she had no inherent worth to herself or anyone else. She could also be a pet who could be used but not really seen for who she was or what she needed. A woman with a pet identity can provide companionship, and sex, and housekeeping, but believes that her own identity is meaningless to anyone else.

Herein lies internalized shame. These erroneous views of Lisa as bad, as deserving to be treated abusively, and only valued for being used are her shame. More accurately, they are the underpinning, the foundation, of her perception of herself. Then cultural shaming and all the unique forms doled out by parents and schools add onto this underlayer. This attachment deprivation causes the deepest, most fundamentally devastating shame.

Attachment in Infancy

A secure attachment in infancy and early childhood provides strength to defend against later shaming. *Our experience of very early life has a powerful effect on our evolving attitudes toward ourselves.* Any child who does not have a secure attachment receives very early shaming. Lisa's mother was condemning of her baby, but it is also damaging for children to receive little or no loving bonding. Evidence for this comes from the study of babies in European orphanages during World War II who died in large numbers even while their needs for food, clothing, bathing, and diapering were being met. When it was understood that they needed to be held and loved and played with, volunteers were found. The babies stopped dying! They needed some sort of attachment, even if inadequate, in order to just stay alive.

Imagine what it would be like to have everyone around you
think you were unlovable, and unloving, and had nothing to offer.
What would you think about yourself?

Shaming in adult life is different from shame coming from attachment deprivation. If someone points out that you have done something shame-worthy, you have the chance to feel that shame, assess if it is appropriate, let the shame flow around in your body, and discharge it. Then it is gone. But when a baby or child internalizes shame, it becomes part of his very identity. Then it stays put.

Instead of a healthy view of oneself as lovable and loving, and growing up to discover gifts and interests, the attachment-deprived baby includes in his picture of himself the way he believes he is seen.

When I think about Lisa's childhood, I know that her mother was miserable, her grandmother depressed, and a baby wasn't welcomed. But Lisa, as the baby, couldn't understand that she had been born into a defective environment. Babies and children, and many adults, are compelled to believe that the way they are perceived is truly who they are.

Of course Lisa's mother didn't want to feed her and hold her affectionately, except on occasion. She wasn't equipped to love a baby, particularly when she blamed the baby for what she had gone through.

The grandmother was happy with Lisa as long as Lisa didn't complain or need anything she couldn't easily give. Lisa's fondest memory is sitting at the kitchen table eating cookies and drinking tea and milk. Lisa could feel good and loved when her grandmother was having a pleasant experience with her.

When the child of disturbed, distracted parents looks to them for love, he is going to feel wrong, not wanted, outside, unloved, unlovable and unloving because the parent is unable to attend to him. This shame comes from how attachment figures relate with him, not just from shaming directed at him. This deprivation of love and attention is far more shaming than statements and looks. He perceives it to be about who he is.

Attachment Theory began with the study of children separated from parents during the child's hospitalization. The outcome has changed policies regarding the role of parents in hospitals. *Becoming Attached* (Robert Karen) describes the history of the research and the social outcomes. (Of course our intuition can tell us everything the research learned, but our shame-based denial of the truth of being human had to be overridden by research.)

When mothers are trying to not experience their shame by distraction or defense mechanisms or other maneuvers detailed in Chapter 8, they diminish their ability to know what we, as children, need and who we are. They are distracted from the child, too. So they may have to fall back on imitating how other mothers act, or follow rules about being a good parent. They may go to books to "learn" about parenting, cut off from their inborn knowing of what is right for a child.

Shame will keep a mother or father from communing with their child. If the child has no one to commune with, he will make up that it has something to do with him. If we come into the world unloved or poorly loved, we believe that we aren't lovable. This becomes an emotional experience. *Believing one is unlovable is a very clear cause of internalized shame.*

Children make up reasons for not receiving appropriate responses to their needs. They assume that it means something negative about them. Once we engage in healing from attachment deprivation, we can examine unmet needs from childhood that we erroneously believe are current needs.

Attachment Styles

Attachment Theory has named four basic styles of attachment: secure, anxious, avoidant, and ambivalent. All of us experience a combination. We may have one dominant attachment style from which we operate most of the time, and another form that operates in certain relationships or situations.

Secure Attachment

Children automatically form a secure bond to the primary caregiver when she or he is emotionally available to the child. Research described in *Becoming Attached* by Robert Karen demonstrated how these children feel safer when exposed to new situations. They have less stranger anxiety and can more freely engage in developmental tasks.

Lisa had no attachment with her mother, but did have the constant presence of her grandmother. This constancy provided physical security, but that is only one component of what a child requires. It was also necessary for Lisa to have her needs accurately perceived and met, which didn't happen. Her grandmother saw her role as stepping in and taking over an obligation that really belonged to her daughter. She felt put upon and resentful for having to care for a baby at her age and while she was struggling against depression.

Anxious Attachment

A child whose mother gives love and meets his needs, but is inconsistent, or from whom he is separated for a time, may develop an Anxious Attachment. This is the clingy, needy child who often has difficulty starting school or staying with sitters. When shamed or criticized in older childhood, she reacts strongly with shame. She feels shamed by the mother's negative or neglectful treatment, and then may be shamed for the resulting insecure behavior. The very expression of an Anxious Attachment brings even more shame!

As adults these people may become overly dependent on a spouse and over-value the experience of falling in love. A threat to the bond with the spouse triggers the early childhood memory of being dependent on the parent (now spouse) for their very survival.

Lisa formed an Anxious Attachment to her grandmother and her mother. She was tossed into the confusion of being told that one woman was her mother—her primary caregiver—yet that woman was gone most of the time. The person who gave her the most attention and met her physical needs was seen as a secondary caregiver with less responsibility. This was confusing, especially when Lisa clung anxiously to her grandmother even while her mother was present. She wasn't comfortable with this woman who seemed to play a major role in her life but had no interest in her.

Avoidant Attachment

Babies who are inundated with attention that isn't based on their needs, or who are controlled to fit the parent's definition of successful parenting, or defined as bad or unwanted, may elect to avoid attachment rather than give in to an incorrect definition of themselves. Instead of clinging for physical survival, they *pull away for the survival of their unique selves.*

These are the babies who push away when held on a lap, who play quietly by themselves for a long time, who may even prefer not seeing their mothers, instead listening from a distance.

An avoidant child must withdraw from the family in order to maintain a sense of her separate, whole being. She is responding to the human fear of losing who we are, second in significance to fear of abandonment. She elects to maintain her own gifts and sense of self. However, as she pulls away, she may be giving up the shreds of love that are available.

As adults, avoidant attachers may be loners, preferring to limit time with others or to be alone. Others may be leaders or CEO's, in positions of power or control that put them at a distance from people. The pain that this separation causes often brings an intense need for a loved one, along with difficulty being with that person. A man may seek a mate for the bond that wasn't possible with his mother, but then pull away as intensely as he sought it.

Avoiders try to avoid internalizing shame, but fail. I grasped onto avoidant attachment to prevent taking on the definition of myself as evil. It didn't avoid all shame, though. Shame is associated with the very need to pull away from other humans. The child wonders what is wrong with him that he can't fit in and belong.

If Lisa had faced only her grandmother's tolerant caretaking, she may have developed just the Anxious Attachment. But her mother's condemnation forced her to pull away from relating in order to maintain a sense of her right to be alive. Lisa seemed to have developed Anxious and Avoidant Attachments at the same time.

I was grateful to have studied Attachment Theory in graduate school because it helped make sense of so much of my childhood, as well as my adult ways of handling the memory of it. Avoidant Attachment was the only intelligent approach to that childhood, even if it meant isolation while living in a family of five. When a child is defined as evil and harmful, the only rational response is to avoid attachment in order not to believe the definition. Though I was depressed as a child, and fell back into it when my son was born, it would have been worse if I had accepted my mother's definition of me.

What would I have done if I saw myself through her eyes? I could have been one of those people with no conscience, who thought nothing of manipulating others to get what I wanted. Why would I hesitate? I would have lost my humanness if I accepted the definition of myself as evil.

Healing Avoidant Attachment has been unnerving because when I first developed it, this approach kept me human. I retained a sense of the rightness of life. My Feet were the source of understanding how it was right to live. Somewhere in the twisted thinking that arises out of crazy definitions of ourselves came the belief that I couldn't ever give

up Avoidant Attachment. After all, it saved me from a horrible existence, or perhaps even death—like the orphans.

My co-healers who are also healing from the need to avoidantly
attach work with me to examine the countless small ways it influences
our relating with others. Our habits have to be examined for their original purpose, and by seeing them, we can let them go. A small example
was my belief that after leaving two early morning voicemail messages
for a co-healer, I can't leave any more. The fearful belief developed in
my childhood was that I was asking too much, I would be boring, and
she would be angry. If she felt put upon, she would do something, I'm
not sure exactly what, but it would be intolerable.

Ambivalent Attachment

Some children switch back and forth between anxious and
avoidant forms of attachment depending on what is going on, and who
they are with, as Lisa did. The adult form can be seen in the person
who is frightened of losing a lover when the lover creates distance, but
feels overwhelmed with the lover who wants a lot of closeness.

Trying to Address Attachment Deprivation

One of my sexually addicted clients had been sick as a baby, and
separated from his mother. Typically, babies and young children have a
difficult time re-engaging in the bond that was present before separation. My client's addiction is focused on getting attention, and saving
others, and not being forgotten. He interpreted his mother's abandonment to mean that he had been forgotten, he was deprived of
needed attention, and he believed that if he had been able to save others,
he could have been valuable enough to be kept. How the infant mind
makes up these things is difficult for the adult intellect to understand.
However, for the purpose of healing it is useful to accept that this is
what a baby does.

The basic trust my client had for his mother that she wouldn't
leave him was damaged after he was sent to the hospital. Thereafter he
searched for a way of relating in which he will never be forgotten.

John Bowlby, the father of Attachment Theory, explains how children can't complete the grief process because their instincts tell them that if they let go of the parent (or a present-day stand-in), they will die. Back in hunting and gathering days, this was true. If the mother wandered off and forgot the baby, he would, of course, die. He needs to have his mother as attached to him as he is to her. The baby will express the *anger component of grief* in order to call out to the mother or her replacement. If no one comes forward, if for example he is truly abandoned, then he can complete the *sad, letting-go emotion of grief and die.*

My client was trying, with adult behavior, to make infant sense of why he had been left. Perhaps if he thought his mother was dead, or the abandonment was irreversible, he would have died. By thinking it had something to do with what he had done, he could nurture hope of changing so that she would return. We can't know for sure, given his memory of that age, but we can make guesses that allow him to heal when they resonate with his emotions. He needs to cry. Now it is safe.

This man feels deep shame. More than the fear of dying from the loss of the maternal bond, he grew up with negative feelings about his face and body and people's interest in him. This is in spite of the fact that he is an attractive young man, and a well muscled athlete. He has lots of friends, but doesn't develop the relationships. His social time is spent flirting with women to get attention. He can't obtain that intensity from friendship. Then he has to impress each woman with sex so she won't ever forget him. He masturbates to fantasies of women he has sexually pleased.

His intense attachment to sexuality signifies that some kind of abuse might have happened in childhood. Research has shown that most sex addicts were sexually abused. However, the severity of his experience of abandonment can account for the use of sexuality to recreate the intensity of the needed childhood attachment. He experiences it as life-saving.

The shame came from his explanations of the abandonment. He medicates shame with the drug of intense, sexual attention. They are laced together now. With experience in treating sexual addiction, I am guiding him through looking at it and working toward change. And I focus on the shame that came from the temporary loss of his mother. He has a great deal of grieving to do for not having had a constant attachment. Grieving for babyhood loss is long and deep—and possible. First he has to understand what happened. Then he has to give himself permission to grieve for what he can no longer remember. And he gets to perceive how he ameliorates shame with sex, and tries to use sex to recreate what he lost.

Attachment abuse in childhood
causes internalized shame.

The culture defines abuse as physical, sexual and emotional, but the form of abuse that is interwoven with attachment can be even more severe. *Attachment is the original need of infants, and remains with us through life as the need for community.* Avoidant Attachment can be seen as a form of isolation that resembles shunning even though the child is making the choice.

Shunning is a harsh form of community punishment—we aren't intended to accept Avoidant Attachment as a way of life.

Parental shunning, known as the "silent treatment," is as devastating as beating. It is a silent statement of the child's lack of acceptability in the family. Trying to make sense of the pain, the child will accept the implication that he or she is not wanted, needed, loved, or doesn't belong. Developing an Avoidant Attachment is one way to ward off the horror of this parental reaction.

The next chapter, Three Stories of Acculturated Shaming, offers examples of different kinds of attachment and how they influence the child's shame level as he or she grows up.

Chapter 3
Three Stories of Acculturated Shaming

In order to exemplify everyday shame that impacts all arenas of our lives and our communities, I am going to narrate the stories of three fictitious people. The first, Jack, grew up in a normal, loving family and received the *normalized version of shame.* Jack is one of those men who say they had a wonderful childhood, that their parents did nothing wrong. Childhood can't have caused adult distress. When such men become my clients I walk them back through *the normal shaming* that needs to be healed. They are usually upset over having to find fault with parents who love them. Therapy groups can repeatedly establish that, while their parents really did love them, they passed on shaming from centuries of generations before them.

The second is Diana. She had even less shaming in her first two years than Jack, but sexual abuse added shame of greater impact.

The third is Maria, who began with little attachment, followed by sexual and emotional abuse. She added her own shaming with addiction and an inability to manage life well. While Maria doesn't seem to qualify as the recipient of acculturated, everyday shaming, she does. All those around her kept denying that she was being harmed. Her parents looked good to the community.

These three people are entirely fictitious, although their stories are accurately presented. This is in contrast to the other examples in the book, which are real people but with identifying information changed so they aren't recognizable.

Jack

Jack was born to a couple who wanted a child. Married two years, and in their late 20's, they were glad they were ready for a family and able to conceive. As the first grandchild on both sides, Jack was welcomed by extended family.

When he cried for "no reason" during the night, as babies do, his mother worried about her husband becoming upset. He had to have enough sleep to do well at work. They weren't surrounded by family as were parents in the hunting and gathering days who had help always available. Jack's mother tried to get Jack to stop crying by anxiously rocking and bouncing him. She didn't like it when he wouldn't stop. She angrily whispered that he was a bad boy, didn't he understand that his father didn't like the noise? That he had to get his sleep?

His mother knew that Jack wouldn't understand her words, and her behaviors were well within the norms of our culture. But Jack was picking up on her tone and her body tension, and he had an energetic understanding that something was wrong with him. His only view of life was what his parents reflected, and so he believed on a deeply primitive level that something had to be wrong with him. This was his introduction to shame.

Jack had an advantage over children whose parents are unable to form a secure attachment with them. He could attach securely and feel safe and loved. I explain attachment theory in Chapter 2. When babies aren't provided the love and attention necessary to form a secure attachment, that creates the oldest, deepest form of shame—the belief that one isn't lovable, or deserving of having needs met. Since babies are born with the need for attachment for their very physical survival, without its presence, they are forced to believe that they are undeserving of love and safety—even life itself. They are discard-able, disposable, leave-able. Their brains are very immature and they are entirely dependent; these beliefs are recorded in an intense, non-verbal, non-intellectual form.

Occasionally, Jack's mother left him with one of his grandparents so she could sleep during the day. When she dropped him off, she shook her head and frowned, saying what a difficult child he was, and how good it was to be away from him for a few hours. Jack took in her tone, body tension, and energetic communication. He was too much work, he was a bother. He took on the shame of believing he caused unhappiness.

There were many happy times, too, such as playing patty cake and laughing so hard playing peek-a-boo. He felt wonderful and safe and loved when he was nursing, and when his dad snuggled him up, making soft, cooing noises. They went on picnics, and both parents played with him, smiling and happy.

After Jack learned to crawl, he got into things. His mother swatted him and said, "No!" firmly, and he took that in and used it to begin to monitor his behavior. That was okay. But when she shook her head, frowning, and looking distraught, he felt somehow not right. This was different from learning rules to follow, or breaking them and hearing "no." She seemed to want to get rid of him, to relegate him to his room and leave him alone. She didn't like being around him. Shame penetrated.

When he was two, and his mother dressed him up for a family gathering, he ran outside and fell onto muddy ground, then played with the wet soil. The family was late, and both parents scolded him angrily while changing his clothes. He understood that he should have known. He felt shame for who he was—someone who didn't know. He couldn't guess what they wanted those many times they treated him like a bad boy, a child who wanted to cause problems. He hadn't played in the mud to make them unhappy, he liked mud.

The parents could not see what was going on inside their son's mind because they had been raised the same way they were raising him. They thought their reactions were not harmful, and their frustrations justified. They had grown up in our emotionally cut-off culture, and had lost their own deep sensitivity. They truly didn't know that their shaming frowns were registering, and adding up year after year. Their lost sensitivity was passed onto their child, even though they were dedicated, loving parents.

All parents shame their children.

We can gather together in order to accept this as a fact. We don't need to shame ourselves for it.

When Jack was three and four, his mother was glad that she hadn't used the disciplinary methods her own mother had used. She didn't spank him, she didn't yell at him. She didn't say, "Bad boy!" She thought expressing annoyance was so much better. She didn't know that this conveyed shame. The tone implies that the recipient is just so stupid, so inconsiderate, so needing to be different, even if the words are neutral. She didn't know this. She was pleased that she didn't use overtly harmful methods.

Jack accumulated tiny bits of shame with each comment. His aunt and other adults gave no indication that his mother's tone was not appropriate, and so he had no mirror of the truth. Everyone was in agreement that the treatment was right. If he had heard one adult tell his parents that they were shaming Jack, and they needed to learn to stop so he wouldn't take it in, he would have had one accurate mirror. This might have helped him know that his parents were wrong when they shamed him, and he might have taken in less. But the whole culture believes that these parents were appropriate in their discipline, and deserved sympathy for the difficult task of raising a young child.

Jack's parents valued education and taught him many things before he started kindergarten. He loved the attention, and so he worked hard to learn. He couldn't know that formal education was not the direction that would help him discover his gifts and talents. He loved to draw, and move things around to look different. Adults said, That's nice, but they didn't help him develop this fascination. They were unable to perceive that education was their interest, not his. They didn't see that he had interests of his own. This is not because they were selfish, narcissistic people; it was because they were typical products of having lived in our society. Their own shame-based understanding of humanness had been short-circuited by shaming throughout their lives.

As they defended against the feeling of shame
by accepting the cultural mores,
they lost their ability to
know everything about themselves and about their child.

After starting school, Jack was annoyed much of the time. He didn't know why, because he had no accurate mirror of his emotions. When he pouted and refused to do what he was asked, he was met with more shaming. *His parents, so full of love and affection, had no idea why he would act this way.* They had truly done nothing inconsistent with our culture's definition of good parenting.

Jack's annoyance and mild rebellion were his way of claiming his unique self, his developing personality. He had no way to communicate that he didn't like the shaming and control of his development. All he could do was try to refuse it.

When Jack was five, his parents took him on a road trip. Jack didn't like to sit quietly for long periods, and tended to complain. This time he set out to enjoy himself and not complain. He told his parents he was going to do this, and he stopped himself each time he shifted into being negative. This pleased them, and they told him how good he was—he was a good boy.

This evaluation shamed him, too, because it carried with it the implication that if he stopped, he would be a bad boy. What he needed was smiles and support for determining his own task, and the pleasure it brought him when succeeding. This would affirm him.

Even while Jack's parents shamed him many times every day, they also worked hard to help him not feel shame! *Our culture has countless methods to relieve people from this very emotion that it creates.*

Jack's parents told him not to worry about getting only a B in math, they knew he was smart. They explained that he would grow into his long legs. They said, "Oh, don't feel bad, honey," when his friends had a gathering and didn't invite him. If we had no acculturated shame, he wouldn't have valued these de-shaming statements. They would have had no value because he would have had no shame.

By the time Jack was in the first grade he knew how important performance was to his parents, and he set out to get good grades. He succeeded, and they exclaimed over each report card. Again, good parenting according to the culture. But when the child learns what to do to be rewarded, he is distracted from following his intuition and interest in developing himself in ways he was intended. Lucky are the children where the reward matches the child's interests. My family valued education for its own sake, and luckily, education was needed to create the right career and life for who I am. However, they didn't support my education for this reason.

When children conceal their intuition, preferences, emotions, gifts, and personality in order to please parents, they lose sight of themselves.

They will stop knowing what they want through the psychological defense mechanisms of repression or denial. Anger and tears, those vital emotions of grief that are needed to leave the past in the past, are blunted, withheld, ignored and shamed.

When a relative or family friend is sexual with a child, the child will feel shame for having received this kind of attention, and will want to hide it. Even when children are trained to tell parents or other adults if inappropriately touched, they usually don't. Their sexuality has already been so laden with acculturated shame, and the subject so avoided for discussion, that the child can't separate typical acculturated sexual shame from the shaming over behaviors done to them.

Even though he had not been physically or sexually abused, Jack was angry. He didn't know why. His outbursts and hitting other children were, of course, shamed. This increased the amount of shame he internalized while not healing past shaming that caused his behavior in the first place. The school counselor leaned forward, looked him in the eyes, and seriously asked why he hit the other child. Neither she nor Jack understood that there was no present-day answer.

In addition to receiving the rules for goodness from his parents and the school, Jack was taken to Sunday school. There he was taught the Ten Commandments and other rules. He learned that being good was the right way to be. If Jack had not been shamed, he might have discovered that the rules actually agreed with his understanding of how humans get along best. Instead of rules, he would have had reflections of what he knew deep inside. But for a child with layers of shame internalized into his very identity, religion became one more source of shame for making him feel that he didn't fit in with the culture's definition of goodness.

Religion gave him a method of feeling good about himself, too, in spite of his growing sense of badness. By following the rules he could be seen by others as good. Amazing. However, he retained a sense that something was incorrect. But this was better than nothing, better than feeling different from others. Jack became a "good boy."

Along with all children, Jack discovered that he could inhibit shame by doing certain things. His parents had modeled rationalizing—it wasn't my fault, I didn't mean to. But this didn't go very far in getting rid of this horrible emotion. Over time he learned that if he shamed other people, he would stop feeling it himself. He started with his sister, and when she melted into a crying puddle, he felt powerful. He didn't like to hurt her, but his need to get rid of shame was strong enough to make it worthwhile. Then he repressed his guilt by believing that she deserved his shaming, and that she was too weak to take it.

Next, he shamed his friends. Soon he discovered that three friends liked to shame others, too, and they aligned with each other. The four boys became mild bullies, laughing at how easy it was to humiliate people. They even shamed their parents. They watched to see what made them feel bad, and then went after it. Jack made his mother feel like a bad mother, and his father a failure in his career, even though he wasn't. He held up high standards, then criticized them for not measuring up. With sarcasm he said, "Dad, now tell me, why didn't you get that promotion? Are you sure it wasn't that you just weren't good enough?" To his mother, "Mom, I know you try hard to cook, but what is this stuff?" Both parents began hating him, but couldn't let themselves know it. They knew it was wrong for their son to speak to them like this, and they had no idea why he did.

Jack diminished his guilt by rationalizing that his parents were inadequate human beings who needed to be spoken to this way. However, he couldn't override his need to please his dad by going to college and majoring in engineering.

By the time Jack reached puberty, his sexuality had been shamed, even though his parents tried to be accepting. From infant erections, to the age three delight in his penis, to the age four sexualized longing for his mother, to the sexual shame projected from all those adults who were feeling their own, he felt shame the first time he masturbated. Normal childrearing in this culture creates sexual shame in everyone. Instead of being amazed by the strong sexual feelings, the erection and the ejaculation, he was mortified. He immediately knew that this powerful experience had to be kept secret. His male instinct to perpetuate the species prevented him from giving up sexuality in order to avoid the shame. So he continued to masturbate, even though each time more sexual shame was layered over the last.

On some deep, unconscious level, Jack resented having to hide his sexuality. So he showed off around his peers. They joined together by joking and looking at girls' body parts and making lewd comments. This acculturated male behavior is one way to angrily push back the shaming! He'd show them how he wasn't going to give in to feeling bad, he'd do what they didn't like and there was nothing they could do about it! He felt powerful and shame-free. But each time he went back to himself, a little more shame had been layered on. This pushed him to again be boldly rude and obnoxious to turn off the dreadful emotion.

Jack's innocent, loving parents had no idea why their son acted like this. They ascribed it to his age, saying teens are like this, he will outgrow it. If they had taken Jack to a counselor, the counselor might very well have agreed, and assisted the family in handling present-day conflicts. Things might have gotten better, but the internalized shame would not be addressed. Parents can't understand that their children are reacting to normal parental behaviors. They don't know that those actions are harmful.

Jack knew on some level that it was a matter of integrity for him to be angry and rebellious. He was punishing his parents for hurting him, which was pointless and didn't change anything. But if he had apologized, he would have felt more shame, as he would have taken on responsibility for the family problems. Either way, his shame would multiply. The lack of understanding of the role of shaming from birth, and in every facet of our lives, leaves all families unable to understand their children's problematic behavior, and unable to find solutions.

Jack did well in school in order to make his parents happy and proud. He had a series of relationships, but as each woman sought to change him in some way, he became angry. Over time he found fault until either she or he ended the relationship. He thought all women must be bitches, and started thinking he might never marry. Again, his parents couldn't make sense of this because they had modeled a good, solid marriage, and assumed he would follow suit. It made no sense to Jack or anyone around him that he was combating shame. He tried to avoid feeling it by staying away from shamers, or by being really good, or by shaming and attacking others. He didn't have to feel it when he won in a competition or got all A's or got drunk with the guys. He achieved relief from shame—this dreadful controller of life. Of course he had to cut himself off from a good deal of his humanness in order to not feel shameful, but it was worth it. He didn't yet know that he could feel the shame, let it move through him instead of stagnating, and discharge it. He could heal it. He could reclaim his humanity.

When turning thirty, Jack fell apart. He hated his engineering job and dreamed about following his interest in art. He was constantly angry, finding fault with everything. He joined a therapy group and gradually came to recognize the normal, acculturated shaming that had dominated his childhood. At last he heard a roomful of people agree that his childhood shaming had been harmful. Once he could grieve it out, he began to smile and laugh. He saw how he had accumulated shame, how he had internalized it, and how he had defended against experiencing it.

Because Jack had a secure childhood attachment with his mother, and was well loved by many, his progress was rapid. Adults who have been seriously abused take more time when relieving the various forms of shame and trauma. In a few months Jack could look at people around him and recognize when they were shaming each other. He could identify reactions to the shaming—the defensiveness, the circular arguments, how TV commercials showed women shaming men, "friendly" put-downs, gossip, and the rest of the list itemized in Chapter 8.

Next he was able to see what he did to not feel the shame, to defend against it. He could gradually stop, let the shame emerge, and discharge it forever. At last he could understand the role of the culture, and how his beloved parents had unknowingly passed its rules on.

Jack was able to tell his parents that he was going to art school, and that if he wasn't financially successful with art, that would be acceptable to him. A year later he started dating, and quickly saw which women would continue to shame him even after he told them not to. He found a woman who was interested in learning about cultural shaming so she could stop, too.

Diana

Sexual shame is a powerful force, as I have described. It inhibits the loving use of sex, and can distort the life of people who are otherwise not highly shamed.

Diana was forty-two when she entered a therapy group. Her children were grown, and she was trying to understand why her life felt somewhat empty. She woke with nightmares of being held down and not being able to breathe. She had never encountered anything like this before and couldn't make sense of it. Her physician prescribed anti-depressants, but she didn't want to take them. She wanted to understand what was happening to her, and what she might do about it.

Her therapist saw her individually for several months before recommending group therapy because she could see that Diana's shame about her sexual relating was too strong to be able to reveal it to others. As they examined the dreams and the body memories, it became clear that Diana had been sexually abused in early childhood. She was able to take the cloudy film off old memories, and realize that she had been molested by an uncle who had lived on and off with her family.

Diana's marriage had gone along smoothly by the standards of the culture. She and her husband had figured out how to solve problems, and both complained to friends about the other instead of engaging in painful circular arguments. Diana had sex with her husband because she believed this was required of her as a wife. But a few years earlier, when her distress began to mount, she could not bring herself to be sexual in any way.

Like Jack's, Diana's parents were loving and affectionate and wanted all three children. Both enjoyed the activities of children at different ages, and their lives were richly defined by family. They provided secure attachments and were able to see and support their children's interests and abilities.

Diana encountered shame later than Jack. Her mother, Fran, had a lot of help from sisters and her own mother. She was able to sleep when needed, which gave her an unusually good experience of new mother-hood. Two sisters had children and could understand what she was going through. They listened well. Diana's father, Richard, was so happy to have a second child, a girl after a boy, that he was glad to go home right after work and be with them. Neither parent was upset over dirty diapers or the baby's crying as they had been with their first. The second was so much easier compared with the shocking life changes the first brings. Their pleasure made it unpleasant for them to shame the baby, and also to shame each other! Diana got off to a good start.

When Diana was old enough to discover that touching her geni-tals felt good, and she lit up, both parents said nothing. They had read that the child should not be stopped or scolded. They couldn't know that their discomfort over watching a child stimulate herself was trans-mitted anyway. Since all people carry sexual shame, whether they are aware of it or not, they cannot help transmitting it to their children. When I ask clients how their parents taught them about sex, almost everyone says that it wasn't talked about. Most of the parents who did talk about it did so in unhealthy ways. I almost don't believe it when someone describes a good history of communication about sexuality.

The only time most people can talk about sex is if engaging in it, or when integrating shame into the discussion: calling sex bad, dirty, nasty, poking the other in the ribs and laughing. Joking. Did you get some? I got lucky. And on and on.

Sex is not an ordinary subject in everyday conversation. It is rare to hear someone say something like, My husband and I had really nice sex last night. We were both relaxed, and it just unfolded naturally into a good bonding exchange.

Parents can believe that by saying nothing they are communicat-ing nothing. But babies pick up energetic communication, and older children understand when something is out of bounds for discussion.

When Diana was three, her uncle who was in college came to live with the family in order to save on expenses. He was a shy young man, so when he discovered that his niece was warm and loving, he appreciated it. He offered to baby-sit when the parents wanted to shop or go out to dinner.

Diana loved the attention of this man who lived with them, this member of her family. She snuggled with him while they watched TV, and followed him around when he worked in the yard or did his wash. She trusted him.

One day when she sat on his lap, he found himself becoming aroused. At first he was shocked, but he had no lover and he missed contact like this. So he moved her body to increase his arousal, thinking she wouldn't know what he was doing. When she wanted to get down, he held on to her because he became focused on his arousal and not her needs. As she fell forward to get off his lap, he caught her by the neck, his focus now on his coming orgasm. He didn't know she was crying and fighting him.

Once he lost arousal after orgasm, he realized what he had done. He put her down and ran to his room where he changed his clothes. He was horrified. He became sullen and quiet.

Diana didn't like having her uncle treat her badly, but she could have bypassed that trauma because of her love for him. But having him withdraw from her and the family was devastating. She thought he stopped loving her. She was afraid he was leaving. So she sought him out, holding his hand and trying to get him to look at her.

The parents watched their brother turn away from the little girl, and they felt sorry for her. They talked with him about spending more time with her, asking what was wrong that he didn't like her anymore. He couldn't explain, and he couldn't change the feelings.

A week or so later, the parents were gone for a couple of hours, assuming it would be good to leave Diana with him. This time when she tried to touch him, she reached for his penis since this had been important to him. He became aroused, and again held her on his lap until he reached orgasm.

Diana was torn between getting attention, and losing him to his sexual trance. If this was the only way she could get attention, she might do it again. But she felt really icky when he did that thing. And she felt bad about herself afterward. Her sexual shame, and his shame, and the way he disappeared from their real relationship were very up-setting. When her uncle moved out of the house two weeks later, she missed him terribly but was relieved to not struggle between wanting him and not wanting the sexualized relating.

In nursery school that fall Diana shied away from men who came to get their children or who worked there. When her parents noticed this, they wondered what was going on in the school, and moved her to a different one. Over time, Diana reacted less and less.

When she became a teenager, she was puzzled over the contrast between wanting the attention of boys but not wanting to get close. Her sexual feelings brought her back to that long-ago experience. It was no longer a picture-memory, so she couldn't connect her teen experience with what happened when she was three. She didn't date until she was in college, and then she advanced slowly. At the same time, she yearned for physical contact with a man she liked. She wanted that sexual feeling and touch. But along with desire came sexual shame.

She met Ted her second year of college and fell completely in love with him. She knew he was a perfect mate, and so she had to become sexual. At first she had several drinks before even kissing. She was terrified as clothing gradually came off. With weeks of working up to it, she calmed her fears by sexual arousal and committing to this man. She was not aware that sexual shame had become embedded into her being from the interactions with her uncle.

Ted felt the same way about Diana, and so was patient with her sexual issues. He knew it was more important to bond into a couple than to have good sex because she was a compatible mate. He wanted to marry her when they were out of school.

They had sex regularly. Diana set no limits as she knew she had issues that weren't his fault. She had orgasms, and experienced pleasure, but if Ted were on a business trip she was relieved to avoid sex. She didn't question this. It just seemed to be the way she was.

Children and her career occupied her, and she went to church to understand how it was right to live her life. She believed she was a good person and hadn't accumulated negative feelings about herself. Her general internalized shame was mild compared with the average person's, but her sexual shame was high. This was more or less avoided by seeing sex as something she needed to do and was all right to enjoy.

The emotions that emerged when she was forty-two were shocking. She knew she needed to do something about them. Her therapist specialized in sexuality and could quickly see that her issues had to do with sex. In asking about Diana's childhood, not just the sexual parts, the therapist was able to discover the presence of the uncle who went from being deeply loving to distancing himself. She understood why people do this and slowly elicited Diana's memory. Because Diana was three, she had no clear picture of the sensation of the erect penis against her, or the hand on her throat. She did have the body memory of both, because she couldn't tolerate having her neck touched, or sitting on a man's lap. Her therapist took her back to those discomforts several times, and each time Diana cried or raged against her uncle. In several months she was freed from the memories and could think of them without much emotion.

Next, her therapist worked toward touching Diana's throat. First she extended her hand, and let Diana have the fear that emerged. Finally, Diana was able to allow her therapist to gently touch her throat. She cried with relief and amazement. A similar process with her husband resulted in being able to sit on his lap, and finally do so when he had an erection.

Diana's progress was rapid because her overall level of shame was low. Therapy could focus on sex. Usually when addressing sexual abuse, people have to address other sources of shame, and the devastating feelings caused by the parents' lack of protection. Diana did this, but it went quickly because she had had a secure attachment with both parents, her relationship with them as an adult was strong and loving, and she had a solid, loving relationship with her husband.

Diana was grateful to be relieved of the emerging emotion memory, and just as glad to discover a true interest in sex. What had been a duty became a pleasure. She felt as if she were falling in love with her husband again as she hadn't been able to use sexual energy and activity in her initial bond with him. A low-shame person himself, he could join her in this new experience of their marriage.

Julie

Julie's history is more typical of what therapists encounter. Not only did her stepfather molest her, he blamed her for it by saying that she was too attractive to him and made him do it. He also shamed her for not being attractive enough. This man was too narcissistic to understand her feelings and needs. He wasn't capable of love and had no way to perceive what was going on. His own shame required high use of denial and alcohol to continue living his life. He couldn't afford to understand his stepdaughter's feelings because if he did, his shame would mount to unacceptable levels.

Julie's mother oriented her attention to her troublesome second husband, terrified that if she didn't take good enough care of him, he would leave, too. Her despair was so strong that she couldn't afford to know what her daughter needed. If she had, she would have felt immense shame and would have had to take action to protect her. She was too terrified to let herself know what was going on. She turned away, basically giving her child to her husband to do with as he pleased.

Shame from sexual abuse was added on to Julie. Shame from the lack of love and caring that Julie took to mean she wasn't lovable or deserving was further compounded by criticism from both parents. They wanted to avoid their shame for how they parented. Criticizing is a powerful way to avoid one's own shame by seeing the other one as shame-worthy.

School was hard for Julie, and so she felt stupid, furthering her shame. She wasn't able to pay attention in class or when reading because she daydreamed about the future. She used the psychological defense mechanism of dissociation to avoid pain. Dissociation can be emotional, intellectual, or physical, or all three. When intellectually dissociated, Julie couldn't learn facts. Her brain wouldn't allow it.

Reaching puberty and discovering strong sexual feelings, she was confused. These were the bad feelings, yet they felt good. As she developed, her stepfather laughed at her body, while her mother feared his attraction would be stronger for the girl than for herself. The already bad dynamics became worse.

Then magic happened. Boys started looking at Julie's body and became really interested in her. Attention of any kind felt good, and she was already accustomed to sexualized attention. She quickly learned how to flirt and dress in provocative ways. Power came from choosing one boy and making it clear to the rest that they didn't qualify. She had intercourse when she was thirteen.

By the time Julie reached high school she discovered the price to be paid for using sex this way. She was placed in the slut category by other girls. They shamed her, adding one more layer. Being used for sex by boys had already compounded her stepfather's conveyance of shame.

Julie started drinking when fourteen, and added drugs as the years went on. She had to use more and more to keep the shame at bay. She wanted to avoid tremendous anxiety and depression that she sensed was right there waiting to grab her.

When a child becomes promiscuous, and drinks and uses drugs, people wonder what is wrong with her. Why does she have hangovers, why does she go out with many boys, why why why? In the last two decades it is better understood that sexual abuse can cause such symptoms, but first the child has to tell.

A twenty-eight-year old woman came to me in 2009, still apologizing to her parents for drinking and using drugs in her teen years, and not obeying their rules. She felt bad for the trouble she caused them! She saw me after she told her parents that her grandfather had molested her from the time she was seven until she was eleven years old. She couldn't tolerate being around him at family gatherings, and her life had been in upheaval.

Julie's stepfather was a professor of engineering at the local university. He was highly respected for his research and teaching ability. Her mother was a fifth grade teacher appreciated by her colleagues and parents. No one would have suspected what Julie was going through. Most didn't believe it when they learned. They took the parents' side.

Somehow Julie managed to get into a local college, but had difficulty getting to classes because of staying out late and having hangovers. Finally, she felt so terrible that she seriously wanted to die. Deep shame for her behaviors along with feeling unlovable, unwanted, and merely something to use, were too much. She started saving anti-depressants that hadn't relieved her depression, and planned to consume them with a lot of alcohol.

While she was planning her death, her mother called. She had finally ended the marriage, and wanted Julie to come home for the weekend to take care of her. Julie felt a wash of rage, and screamed into the phone. She told her mother that she had never been taken care of, that her mother had stayed with this horrible man who abused her and did nothing about it, and that, no, she wasn't going to take care of a woman who had never been a mother!

She slammed down the phone and threw the medication down the toilet. Storming out of her room, she charged across the campus to the counseling center. With more energy than she had felt in a very long time, she demanded that the receptionist give her someone to talk to right then. She was escorted to an office, and poured out the story of her whole miserable life.

With the help of the counselor, she went to A.A., and got support in giving up the chemical method of avoiding shame. She felt amazingly good as her body healed from the assault. Her counselor warned her that the shame would emerge once she stopped using these ways of avoiding it. Sure enough it did. But nothing was worse than feeling suicidal. She responded well to support for righteous anger at both parents, even while this did not include expressing it directly. It was clear that they were both so disturbed, they wouldn't be able to give her the response that she needed to assist healing.

The combination of shame beginning with being unloved, then compounded by being sexually abused, then overlaid by ongoing harsh criticism, left Julie with a great deal of shame to challenge, discharge, and grieve out. She went to therapy for eight years, and continued in a group and A.A. for much longer.

Chapter 4
Sexual Shame

Sex is one arena in which most people are aware of having shame. I wrote about this in a book called *Treating Sexual Shame*. Working with sexual abuse survivors and sex addicts made it clear to me that shame underlies the issues for both, and impedes healing.

I have long offered sexual shame workshops and classes, knowing that if people can learn how to heal this kind of shame, the rest of healing from shame will become easier.

Jennifer came to three workshops before joining a group. She sat through the first one without speaking. In individual sessions, she cried over how amazing it was to hear the other women talk about simple things like first bras and first kisses. She talked about how her heart felt frozen, clutched tightly in her chest even while the women's eyes got brighter and livelier as the hours went on.

Jennifer had been having sex from the time she was fifteen but managed to put it into a compartment separate from the shame that appeared when trying to talk about it. Alcohol helped, even though she wasn't an alcoholic.

Jennifer's terror over the emerging shame supported the need for my guideline that no one has to talk. She was able to tell the other women that she was terrified, which helped them understand and not take her silence personally. They also saw that she listened intently.

When Jennifer was finally able to talk, all of us were surprised by the subject that had brought such distress—until we heard the whole story. When she started her period at age ten, before she had seen the movie about menstruation, she had no idea what the blood on her clothes was. She thought she was bleeding to death. Here's the really shocking part. She couldn't tell her mother! Her very shame at being alive made her believe that her mother would have no interest, do nothing to take care of her, and let her die. Of course her mother wouldn't do any of those things, but Jennifer's experience of being hated and envied so contaminated her self-esteem that she led her life as if needing nothing from her mother. Her sexual shame over the sign that she was becoming a woman was magnified by her perception of her mother's feeling toward her.

I met her mother when she was on a visit. She is a narcissistic woman who could see little beyond herself and her interests. Raising children had to have been challenging as she preferred staying with her own thoughts. Even when the four girls were adults she was unable to see them for who they were. Jennifer became the surrogate mother, taking care of the younger three so their mother wouldn't feel burdened. Yet in this, too, she was seen as a failure.

Jennifer's mother viewed herself as a powerful woman, and in her 70's when we met, she walked with a sense of dignity and strength. Initially this was appealing until it became clear that she was unable to relate intimately at all. Her facial expression of interest in me appeared feigned. I do believe that she had as much interest as she is capable of. The lack of interest wasn't something I took personally.

The price of narcissism is an inability to be interested in others. With this disability, she had to come up with logical reasons why her children did what they did. She had no intuitive understanding. Then, sadly, the children made up that their mother's reactions to them was because of who they were.

This client's story demonstrated the importance of siblings when parents can't love adequately. Jennifer became the parent of girls only two, three, and five years younger than she was, because this was valued by them and their mother. With sexuality already distorted in the family, and the younger girls learning about it from an immature older girl, sexual shame and misinformation were rampant.

When exploring why a workshop on sexual shame seemed fitting when Jennifer's overall shame was strong, she explained that her self-hate revolved around sexuality. Her mother wanted to be the only beautiful female. She flirted with the girls' boyfriends. She shamed them for any evidence of sexuality. Internalized sexual shame doesn't require having been sexually molested. In fact "normal" parents produce degrees of it.

Sexual shame is the most obvious example of passed-along shame. Parents' discomfort with sexuality shows up in an inability to talk about it with their children, in shaming genital touching, and fostering an overall view that sexuality is bad. The culture contributes with words like nasty and dirty, said in a joking or sexual way.

Of the many kinds of workshops I have led, those for women who want to heal sexual shame evolve into the most committed healing groups. Women bond together around this painful subject, gradually revealing—and remembering—events from childhood and adult life.

When addressing this deeply felt shame, women have to have permission to say nothing in front of each other. If a woman feels required to talk, her shame could inhibit being able to. At the beginning of a workshop I bring up subjects such as first bras and first kisses and what parents said about sexuality. I tell my own experiences, and this quickly engages others to want to tell theirs. Shame-healing has a natural draw.

Men want to heal sexual shame, too. But most have a more difficult time taking a look, because they are culturally trained to think that they should be very sexual and have no problem with it. Sex addicts find it easier to heal because they know they have sexual issues. In group therapy their shame emerges, gets talked about, and discharged.

Sexual shaming is unavoidable.

Sexual shaming is universal, incorporated into the culture. Even when parents try their best to talk openly with children, they cannot have healed their own shame sufficiently to not pass some of it on. Even if parents do a fairly good job, peers pass along the shame they received. When figuring out how to date and kiss and engage sexually, children do not have good role models. They are left with rules from adults, unspoken beliefs of parents, and pressure from peers.

Every one of us had shameful sexuality directed at us by television, jokes, high school classmates making lewd comments, gestures and sounds, and now the Internet. Looking at pornography shames the viewer because the culture says this is shameful. And, the actors are conveying "dirty" or "bad" behaviors, as shame has become part of what is arousing. This shame merely adds to the shame already in place, cementing it.

Anyone who wishes to heal must address this intense form of sexual shame that violates our basic humanness.

Shaming from Sexual Abuse

It has long been known in the treatment of sexual abuse that victims take on the shame of their abusers during the molestation or rape. The pedophile or sex addict or other person who crosses sexual boundaries feels shame because society condemns it. When overriding shame, they are able to carry out acts that violate their integrity, but their shame is energetically transmitted to the child in the same way that children pick it up from adults with no words spoken.

The child's own shame about sexuality is already in place before the molestation, which compounds it. When the molester approaches the child, whether it is for rape or gentle fondling, the child already has shame associated with the attitude of the adult. In the same manner that babies interpret lack of love and attention as meaning something about their own worth and lovability, they interpret the sexual at-tention as something they have caused or initiated or agreed to. The molested child's shame is magnified.

We therapists have repeatedly heard how incest survivors weren't able to tell their parents or other adults. We have also heard moth-ers lament over why the child didn't tell, assuring her or him that she would have stopped the abuse. The child's sexual shame level was so high that she couldn't reveal this shameful experience. Even though it was done to her, the shame is still there. Imagine what it would be like as an adult to describe to your mother the experience of oral sex. Ev-ery client I ask about sexual activity is embarrassed, even though they know I specialize in sexuality and have heard it all. Most were unable to talk with other therapists, needing a specialist in order to overcome shame. Then add to this the horror of truly shameful sexual behavior, and it becomes impossible for most children to talk to a parent.

When people are in therapy to heal sexual shame, they have great difficulty addressing what was done to them. It is easier to remember and process beatings and controlling and criticism. These bring shame too, but the level of sexual shame involved in the act added to already existing sexual shame is overwhelming. In addition, if the therapist isn't paying attention to the shame level, educating the client about this major obstacle to healing, and assisting in the reduction, healing can go very slowly. I have long valued holding workshops on sexual shame because it is brought to the forefront. Each member can focus on this most inhibiting experience more easily with other people doing the same. Grief for abuses of all kinds can be more readily accessed.

Multiple research studies have long established that about a third of women and a fifth of men have been inappropriately touched as children. We also know that many severe abuses are repressed or denied. Recent studies indicate even higher numbers.

Given that so many of us had the shame-ridden sexuality of another person projected onto us, starting with healing sexual shame may be a valuable way to focus. Jennifer discovered this, and later broadened her explorations to her childhood attachment deprivation.

Chapter 5
Recognizing Shaming

I set out years ago to learn to recognize when people were shaming me. It's been a slow education as our culture built shaming in as a normal, natural and right reaction. Since shaming is the cause of the evil in the world, education is vitally important to bring about cultural change. If we can't see when we are being shamed, we will take it in, adding one more piece to the layers. It's easier to refuse what we can see. So we need to see.

Since shaming is so woven into the world, most of it is invisible, the way a picture on the wall is no longer seen. Once we look at that picture, it quickly becomes apparent. Subtle shaming remains fuzzy and out of focus until we have observed it long enough to see it with magnification. Only the more obvious comments are seen, such as: What's wrong with you? How could you do that to me? Shame on you! You're so stupid!

While a couple stood waiting for their drinks at Starbucks, the woman spoke to the man in a quiet, constrained voice as she explained why she wasn't going out with him that evening. The people he wanted to be with were drinkers who became abusive as the evening went on, she explained. These words could have conveyed no shame, but her tightly held mouth, frown, and rigid body made it clear to me that she hated him for even suggesting that she should go. Her shaming indicated that he shouldn't go, too.

The man defensively defended his friends, saying that they could leave if anyone seemed drunk, that if it went on he didn't want to stay either. His tone communicated that she was horrible for treating him as though he were thoughtless and inconsiderate.

My editor thought about how to convey the difficulty of seeing what is going on right in front of us by mentioning how we no longer see pictures hanging on our walls after they have been there for a time.

This is a good metaphor, yet not adequate. Once you stop and look at the picture, you can see it again. With much shaming going on all around us, people will actually not see it even when it is pointed out. When giving talks on shame I have found that when I describe shaming, or ways that people avoid feeling shame, arguments can start!

To continue this metaphor, the other customers didn't notice the picture on the wall. Their interaction was entirely within the norm. One or two people might have curiously looked over, seen that there was a picture hanging there, but it would be out of focus and fuzzy, colors all run together. They would be unable to see the harm being caused. It would be no more than something going on by the stand, nothing more than a couple with a conflict.

Shame healers would be aware of so much more. They would hear the tone, look over, and bring into focus the experience of the man being shamed. They would see that the woman couldn't have a boundary and not go out with him. She couldn't express a preference that he not go too. And he couldn't ask her to just tell him what she wanted without having to see him as thoughtless, unkind and selfish.

Join me in fine-tuning a perception of shaming that is invisible to the acculturated eye.

Shame woven into normal conversation addresses all levels of our identity. Our physical, emotional, mental, spiritual, social, behavioral and lifestyle facets are all condemned all the time. Then the internalization of such shaming makes us believe that we are basically bad, and must follow certain rules to be seen as good.

Physical shaming includes shaming body functions. A woman talking to other women in a gym locker room puts her husband down for snoring. Women compare each other's bodies to see where each rates. All agree that being overweight is shame-worthy, along with having flab, cellulite, and wrinkles. Women diet, thinking their self-esteem will arrive when they reach the right weight. But the internalized shame doesn't go away. She is still too short, too tall, not the right shape, her skin is imperfect, her head is too small, mouth too big, shoulders too broad. And breasts! It's now easy to pay to get them to look "right."

Mental shaming is passed onto every child going to school. All are evaluated against a standard instead of being helped to develop individual mental interests and gifts. Being below average in intelligence is seen as something to laugh at or condemn. Yet, below average means half of all people. Smart people are shamed, too. Those who consider themselves not smart enough take pleasure when a smart person gets something wrong.

Emotional shaming is commonly called abusive when it's extreme. Ordinary versions include treating someone as if they are inferior, can't love well, don't pay enough attention to their partner, don't interact appropriately with co-workers—anything that makes a person feel bad about themselves. It is a major cause of lack of self-esteem.

Spiritual shaming comes from living in a culture that believes that integrity is something made-up, where rule-following makes you good, where religion means rules to follow. Internalized shame has prevented almost everyone from knowing how we are designed to interact and our real purpose here.

Social shaming makes social drinking popular. As fear and shame slide away, it becomes possible to have a better time in social situations. People who have difficulty conversing or whose shame prevents them from relating with interest are put down by the very facial expressions of others.

Behavioral shaming exists in athletics where a person is valued for performing well and put down for not. Children are shamed for not behaving, for not being ready on time, for not staying in bed, for fighting with siblings, and lack of obedience.

Lifestyle shaming is reflected in the phrase, "Keeping up with the Joneses." People feel shame, and are shamed, for living on little, and for being too wealthy. Rich people are envied as well as shamed for having too much. No one can create a lifestyle that won't be shamed by someone.

One way to question if you are being shamed is to look at how you feel. This isn't foolproof because people often feel shame when information is delivered shame-free. It's a good place to start, though. For example, while one server in a restaurant may make you feel good as you exchange information about food, another may be indifferent, and you have no reaction. When the third asks for your order, you may have an odd sensation of being put down, or that it's too much work to wait on you, or a bother. Something is wrong with you. If you check this person out, you may get other clues.

In a gourmet Santa Monica restaurant, my friend and I noticed that the woman seating us was rushed, pushing our menus at us before we could even sit down. We sort of fell into our chairs with huge menus in our hands and purses on our arms. The server came over and stood with feet wide apart, head slightly back, staring down at us. I had looked at the menu and seen ingredients I didn't care for, and asked if the sauces could be switched. He frowned, shaking his head slightly, as he explained that the chef had come up with excellent combinations of flavors that weren't to be changed. He acted as though we weren't quite smart enough to understand.

My friend had eaten there many times, and found this treatment very different from what she had come to expect. I guessed that either we weren't dressed properly or the server was afraid of losing his job. She later learned that the chef was worried about the restaurant closing because the economy had reduced his business. The staff was clearly affected by fear, and weren't present to those of us there for dinner.

If we had not seen what was going on, and had taken it personally, we would have consumed a little more shame. Our need to be treated graciously in an expensive restaurant that served a chef's original gourmet dishes wasn't met. The classic response to this treatment is to turn it back on the staff—complain how poorly they treat their customers, they should be fired, how does this place stay in business. Counter-shaming reduces shame.

We needed information in order to not do what babies do— assume it was something we had done or merely who we were. The staff's behavior implied that we weren't worth their attention. This was clearly not true. They needed us. They needed our business and our money. Their fear and impending shame from losing a job and a business didn't allow them to see us—to see our needs. They reacted in their habitual ways of avoiding shame and fear. The hostess was so out of touch with herself that she couldn't perceive how to treat us. We were no more than furniture. Mothers of babies can react the same way for the same reason.

I won't go to the restaurant again. I missed out on one of the experiences of eating an amazing, unique meal—the friendly communing over this experience that enhances the fascination of new flavors.

My friend and I weren't harmed by the shaming because we could see what was going on, know that it was caused by things we didn't understand, and that it truly wasn't about what we wore or the questions we asked.

Some Mexican-Americans in Southern California carry shame as a result of decades of shaming directed toward them. I drove by two men who apparently looked over at me with the assumption that I was a racist and shaming them. When I lived here twenty-five years ago, these people carried such obvious shame I assumed it was characteristic of all Mexicans. When I visited Mexico, I saw an entirely different people! Then I knew that that those in Southern California were suffering from racism. I was deeply pleased when returning here to see that this is no longer true! The Mexican-American population, now with many who grew up here while maintaining their language and cultural heritage, carries comparatively little shame. These men are now the exception.

When a young man with tattoos, piercings and attitude approached the bank teller, she communicated disgust and contempt by her expression and energy. He was uncomfortable being new to banking. He didn't know he needed his card or a deposit slip. He received her silent shaming, added onto the internalized layers. While he may very well have been a gang member who does bad things, I felt sorry for him. I wanted her and everyone to welcome him into the world with genuine caring.

Self-Shaming

After receiving shaming for decades, we fall into a natural shaming of ourselves. If we feel compelled to believe that the culture and parents and others are correct, then it is only natural to turn on ourselves as well. "How could I have done that?" "What was I thinking?" "I'm so stupid." "Can you ever forgive me?" Self-shaming is seen as low self-esteem. It prevents developing one's gifts, completing needed education or training, or other approaches to living fully. Self-doubt, self-criticism, immobility, apathy, and depression are only some of the ways self-shaming inhibits living a full life.

As I studied every sign of shame while writing about it, I noticed one of my own, very ordinary examples. My wood floors quickly go from lovely to layered with cat hair and dirt—the price of having five little creatures living with me. If a close friend drops in I ignore the floor, but if someone I don't know well is coming, especially if they haven't been in my house before, I feel compelled to sweep it. If I don't, then I have to acknowledge to my guests that the floor is a mess. As I wondered why I do that, I saw that I was trying to say that really, I have clean floors, they just aren't at the moment. I'm a cleaner person than this. Please believe me!

Once I saw this, I deliberately observed myself when a friend came over. I deliberately didn't sweep, and just felt the shame. As it flowed out of me, I laughed at the absurdity of evaluating myself based on how much hair was on the floor!

The Victim Triangle

This triangle of victim, rescuer and abuser has been called a variety of names. I think that it might best be called the Shame Triangle. All three positions are designed to inhibit the experience of shame. If you can come to recognize when people are playing parts in this configuration instead of living fully, recognizing shaming will be easier!

Assuming the roles of victim, abuser, and rescuer is not about genuine victimization, or the needed caretaking by those who intervene. Anytime people operate in the triangle, they aren't living in the real present. Emotions are manufactured. All of us can assume any of the three points, but tend to prefer one. Rescue seems the nicest, kindest point, but it is just as false and shame-based as the other two.

Taking any of these three positions is also relevant when studying how we avoid shame by abusing, rescuing and feeling like victims. We can look at it from the position of how we shame others, as well as how we try to prevent being shamed. This single triangle could justify a whole book on shaming and its prevention. Addiction recovery circles understand this determinant of much social relating.

Victim Position in the Triangle

Victim behavior is very common in our culture. Whenever a person complains about something unfair, hurtful, mean, critical, or incompetent, he or she is shifting into a victim mentality. The healthy approach is to discuss issues, problems, and conflicts with the attitude of what can be done to solve them. Anything else is merely a way to pass time. Criticizing the banking crisis, the economy, politicians, bosses, employees, family members, etc., in a manner that doesn't impart information or seek a solution is engaging in victim mentality.

Victim shaming is a common American pastime, often conducted over drinks or coffee or during an evening with friends. Now that I don't join such exchanges, I have become unpopular with those who value them. If I sit and say nothing, others' shame is often triggered. They feel judged by me, even while I am just observing.

To take the victim position is by definition, shaming. If you feel like my victim, then you must see me as harming you—abusing you! If you think I should have called you two days ago, or I should have acknowledged your birthday, or remembered that you are spending the day with another friend, or if in any way you find fault from a victim stance, you will be shaming me. A straightforward approach is being in reality, which might include healthy anger, tears and other emotions. A healthy response will still hold me accountable for actual things I have done that aren't in my integrity, but it won't shame me for them.

When listening to conversations of victims bonding against perceived abusers, I notice that they create a sense of us against them. *What's wrong with them, why do that do that, don't they know anything, why don't they know?* The speakers are righteous, knowing they are right and the people they criticize are wrong. The relief from shame is palpable. They truly feel good.

Being the object of this criticism is painful. For anyone who hasn't healed their internalized shame—almost everyone—overhearing this kind of conversation about you is awful. It can create unforgivable rifts, cause people to not speak to each other for years, and have *arguments with back and forth shame-throwing.* How did that happen?

It is commonly thought that people higher on the value scale receive less shame than those lower down. Poor people feel automatically shamed by the wealthy. The uneducated feel judged by the educated. Employees feel one down to bosses. However, those higher on the scale receive just as much shaming when those lower down adopt the victim stance, feeling abused by those above them merely because they are below them.

A woman working for a former publisher of mine set up a workshop for me to lead, and when it was over, told me that I didn't give her any appreciation. She was shaming me for having done something wrong. If she wanted to know if I thought she did a good job, she could have said, "Anne, are you satisfied with how I handled this?" Then we would have been equals. I could have said, "Yes, you had everything organized and it went smoothly. I hope we get to do this together again."

Victim shaming is perhaps the most difficult to recognize because the victims feel on the receiving end of harm. How could they be the harming one? When their shaming is named, they might again feel victimized, and deliver more shaming.

There are many kinds of victim stances. They include hostile victim, angry victim, powerless victim, needy victim, shaming victim, mean victim, passive-aggressive victim.

Lisa adopted a victim identity for good reason as she was growing up. After the initial lack of attachment, at age four she was brought into the family when her mother married a man who wanted a daughter to be sexual with. Her mother's desperation for a man led her to sacrifice her daughter—perhaps without awareness.

As being victimized graduated into a victim identity, Lisa then assumed critical victim and hurt victim and violated victim stances with the men she married. The first two were abusive, and so from an outside perspective, her shaming made sense. However, when understanding shaming, it can be seen that directing it at husbands not only engendered their rage and abuse, but harm to her, too. She couldn't figure out what she needed and present that in a straightforward, honest way. This would have supported her integrity. The abusive victim presentation, however, left her feeling powerless, while the men felt hideously shamed. A deadly combination.

Lisa's emotional healing included exploring the real powerlessness in childhood, and the shame that came with it. As she grieved it away, she could see how she had tortured her husbands, shaming them, and then suffering their methods of handling it. She could see that understanding her need for boundaries was essential in order to not abuse others. She had to heal her own shame to achieve that.

Fearing Others Shames Them

If people are afraid of you, they are shaming you by seeing you as potentially harmful. They may not know they are shaming, and can't stop if they did. Of the four office managers I have had, three saw themselves as my personal equal, did their work, and got paid. The fourth was afraid of me, feared that I was going to fire her, and was uncomfortable around me no matter how hard I worked to rescue her. I finally gave up, and scheduled so that we weren't very often in the office at the same time. That boundary felt better because I wasn't comfortable being viewed as harmful, or potentially harmful. I believe I would still choose to be near someone who was my equal and not afraid of me.

Triangulated Marriage

Wives commonly take the victim position in marriage, blaming the husband for everything he does wrong. The culture supports her in this, and supports him in taking the shaming. She is the good gender, he is the bad. It also supports him in being passive-aggressive instead of setting boundaries by telling her that she isn't to shame him. As men and women become educated about shame, they have a better chance of forming good relationships. Once shaming is stopped, the opportunity to use healthy emotions to resolve conflicts improves.

Anytime people take a victim stance,
they are shaming others.

Something to Try

Meet with friends or acquaintances you know are likely to discuss politics or religion or the economy or their health. Step back and listen. Notice how their voices change as they engage in a topic with victim-shaming. Do they become more lively? Do they smile? Do they frown with a how-can-they-do-this-to-me quality? Or do they take a how-could-they-be-so-stupid attitude? Do they shake their heads?

Try to not join in. Listen impassively. Does anyone react to you? Do they try to get you to join in? How does it feel to not join them? Do you experience a tug to ward off feeling on the outside? Or judged? If you maintain your listening stance, do they change how they address you? Do they stop triangulating? Do they go on, leaving you on the sidelines? Do they criticize you for being silent? Do they rescue you, perhaps with concern that you aren't feeling well? How do they try to make sense of your behavior?

How do you feel when you don't join in? Is it difficult? Do you want to belong and fit in by doing the same?

A woman I know enjoys putting others down when gossiping. She details others' emotional and physical difficulties. I don't join her in a helpless look at those "poor people" she is describing. For example, I told her that her daughter-in-law with obsessive compulsive disorder would be helped by intensive psychotherapy along with a certain anti-depressant. Even though this woman was speaking to an expert on mental illness, she brushed me aside, saying that the young woman was managing well, and didn't need help.

This woman is dedicated to energizing herself by shaming others, and therefore has no interest in learning how to help them. The intensity of her need to avoid her own shame prevents it. Now if I had felt obligated to step in to control her into helping her daughter-in-law,

I would have shamed her—both with my tone, and by the very belief that she needed to be controlled into being different. Instead I sat back and noticed what was going on, and accepted that there was nothing I could do. That brings freedom. I would recommend that anytime you find yourself with strong feelings about what someone else is doing, first step back and observe. You might still find strong feelings, perhaps some that need to be expressed, such as healthy anger or tears. *The desire to shame others to stop them from shaming may appear!* The task is to just notice all of it.

If you gather your co-healers together to study shame in the presence of shamers, you can devise signals to alert each other to stop and observe. A touch on the arm can communicate. Find words that are meaningful, such as "student," or say the person's name, or look the co-healer in the eye and smile. You may ask your co-healer to speak to the others in order to allow you to step back and observe. See if you can pull your attention back to the study of shame, and away from your reactions to shaming. You can ask your co-healers to do this for you so that you aren't alone in trying to observe your emotions.

When away from the shamers, catalog what went on. Look at how they were medicating their shame. Notice how they felt when you didn't join them. Observe what they did about it. See each example of shaming—toward the object of their conversation, toward you, toward each other. Notice if you wanted to shame anyone. Notice if your shame was triggered, and by what.

This education will lead automatically to change, because it is removing cultural denial of culturally-approved shaming. As long as denial is in place, we can't see, and if we can't see we can't change.

Abuser Position in the Triangle

The very word, abuser, indicates that shame is on the way. This is one point in the triangle that is understandable to everyone. The person who yells at you or criticizes or hits is clearly indicating that you are terrible and deserve such treatment. However, all points in the triangle shame all the others, and so all points are abusing.

There are many kinds of abuse that don't seem abusive by the culture's definition. Passive aggression may be difficult to identify. A client's husband pulled up her beloved tomato plants before the season was over. She sensed that his reasoning that they would die soon was a cover for his desire to express aggression in an unrecognizable way.

Other kinds of hurtful actions are invisible because they are within a societal definition of acceptable, and difficult to describe because cultural denial prevents their being noticed. This is why getting together in a group to watch movies and TV ads, stopping each minute to examine the exchanges for shaming, is needed in order to *remove denial from what is going on all the time. TV ads typically shame someone.* Apple ads for the Macintosh shame the PC representative, even though the Apple rep doesn't shame him. The PC guy expresses his own shame as he attempts to prove that he is superior, even knowing he isn't. We are invited to feel shame if we buy a PC, and to feel genuinely superior and right if buying the Mac.

While I was checking out in a pet store, the manager spoke to the checker in a cold and critical tone. I am sure she would have denied her shaming. She saw herself as a powerful supervisor giving needed information to an underling. The underling hated her and hid it well. Though this situation would be considered by many as harsh, others would think the manager was doing a good job and would assume that the checker deserved it because of poor performance. Before studying shame I would have thought the manager was not very nice, but acting within the norm for her position.

Anytime people are in an abuser stance,
they are shaming others.

All abuse is shaming. Those who have healed from it sufficiently not to feel shame can observe abuse without receiving shame. But for every person who has internalized shame—everyone—abuse hooks up with our beliefs that there is something seriously wrong with us. If we as babies believed we were neglected because of who we are, this same belief will be present in later abuses. Women who are hit and controlled have to struggle to believe that they don't deserve such treatment. Men who are shamed for not doing things correctly will believe the criticism, even while disbelieving it. Both partners then defend against their own shame by shaming the other. Thus is born the circular argument, going around and around with no idea of the original subject. The subject isn't important. The shaming style of the argument is.

Manipulating and controlling others can be difficult to perceive as abuse. A man told his wife that she was controlling when she refused to go sailing with him on a weekend that she chose to spend otherwise. He said that because she wouldn't let him do what he wanted, she was controlling him. The truth is that he was controlling her. He wanted her to do what he wanted instead of respecting her own use of time. By getting her to believe that she was doing something harmful—controlling—he controlled. Over the course of the day as they sailed, she was resentful, refused to do much to crew, and sulked. She couldn't see that he was abusing by convincing her that she was shame-worthy. Yet she knew the truth on some level because she took it out on him. She shamed him in return.

For this woman to have stayed out of this morass, she would have to see that *setting boundaries is not controlling*. She'd have to see the false reasoning he presented as truth in order to control her. If she had known that she was going to make him pay with her attitude, she might have gained the strength to not let him. Even if he were to shame her more, and punish her in some way, she'd experience less shame than what she brought on herself by going along and making him pay for it.

Being Seen by Co-Healers

Studying together with co-healers provides the support of being seen by several people at the same time. In a grocery store when a mother is yelling shaming comments at a child, we are pretty sure that she is hurting him. But no one says anything. The closest people come is to make quiet, side comments to another shopper. While this may peel away some denial, it still leaves us with the sense that this is normal. "Oh my god, look what this terrible person is doing to her child! We aren't like that, are we? I know you aren't, and you can see that

I'm not." Triangulation serves to at least acknowledge that something dramatic is occurring, and we can view it together.

What would it take to truly see that this mother is at her wits' end, she just can't think clearly or care anymore about how she appears? This kid is driving her crazy.

Our culture has a rule that you aren't allowed to speak to the mother, unless you attack her. One man who did was, of course, yelling at his own mother for when he was a child. The woman he told to stop talking that way to her child was with a friend, and they both looked at him as if he was crazy. Other shoppers took his side. Nothing changed in the child's life.

Imagine speaking to the mother. If you were able to observe, to see that she is full of shame, that she has passed this along to the child who now drives her nuts, and that she can't change herself to be a non-shaming mother, then what? Intervening is useless. The child has been harmed, and he will continue to be. There is nothing you can do to help him. What you can do is *grieve for him, for the mother, and for yourself.*

We all need to cry for the shame that has dominated each of us and the sadly limited world we live in.

Perhaps it can help to know that your grief ,together with evolving out of a shame-based life, are what you can do to help this child. As each of us purifies ourselves by removing shame, we offer that to everyone around us without having to say a word. I can imagine standing and looking at this mother. No smile. Just looking. Reflecting what I see with compassion. Not shaming her.

It is likely that she will feel more shame if I do this. But I didn't cause this shame. It is layers upon layers of old shame that she is, for a moment, not masking. Perhaps she will receive no benefit, but I will get to live in the truth.

I know that she can't help it, that she needs assistance to heal her shame, that she is programmed by the culture and her family's history to take it out on the next generation. She is carrying it forward. For a moment she will be in the presence of someone who is no longer carrying it on. She has a mirror available of who she really is. I cannot determine if she will use that mirror. All of us who are healing shame can offer up a new view, though. As more and more of us become able to do this, more and more people around us will, too—even without setting out to. We are creating a movement. It is all we can do. It is all we need to do.

Rescuer Position in the Triangle

Rescuing seems to be a very nice thing to do, and so it is a popular choice for those who work to avoid shame, or want to prove that shame isn't warranted.

In contrast to meeting real needs and giving loving gifts, the rescue position in the triangle sets up the giver and the receiver to believe that something real and nice is going on. However,

giving real things for the wrong reason
shames the receiver.

Here are some examples:

A man projects a childhood need for constant attention onto his wife, and shames her if she doesn't meet it. This need isn't real, it isn't valid in the present. He didn't receive attention that was appropriate in childhood, and all he can do now is grieve for the deprivation.

His wife will try to meet his expressed needs for attention and concern though they can't be met. This is a set-up for bad marriages where one member actually tries to do what the mother of the infant did not, instead of learning to differentiate what is truly required in the present.

Some professions have a high percentage of people who feel good about themselves for being able to help. When they attract those who want to feel good about themselves to offset shame, much of the motivation and pleasure comes from reducing shame. And, much of the "help" isn't what the patient actually needs, but instead what will make the helper feel good in the short-term.

Those people who are so very nice, smiling and acting as if you are a good friend when you have just met, are offering a rescuer false self. The man who spoke lovingly of his father and brothers, effusing over how important they are to him, then revealed that the contact with his brothers occurred on holidays and birthdays, and his father on a monthly schedule. After his mother left when he was five, he was the family rescuer. His rescuer emotions continued even though he stopped the behaviors.

My mother spoke warmly with a smile to all people, then gossiped behind their backs. Many actually thought she cared for them.

One of my co-healers has a brother who spends a lot of time in victim, lamenting how his mother violated his childhood, and that the world is against him. When his sister responds as if she can help him, she gets frustrated because, in trying to rescue, she fails. Whenever she offers help to co-healers it is powerful and full of love. That's because we can accept real help, while her brother can only ask for rescue from a victim stance.

From the time she was a small child, a client was trained by both parents to rescue them. They acted helpless and needy, and made her feel guilty if she didn't put their needs first. Guilt played in her adult life, as she believed that rescuing her husband and friends was the only way to be of value. Fending off guilt when setting boundaries and meeting only real needs was difficult because both parents had done such a thorough job of training her. First she had to stop rescuing them. Both had homes, jobs, friends and social lives. It was difficult to grasp that taking a rescuer stance with these adults, now in their 60's, was actually putting them down because it was based on the assumption that they couldn't take care of themselves. They, too, believed that they couldn't, even while both did.

Lisa learned to rescue because it was the only way she managed to get attention from both her mother and grandmother. It was a valuable way to get results when natural ways weren't effective. Although neither woman was able to openly love the child, they did appreciate when Lisa served them. She quickly discovered what both women liked, and then offered it as often as it could be received.

As the mother of adult children, for a long time Lisa believed that her value to them was to give and give. This is a classic example of projecting what was true, or believed to be true, in childhood onto one's adult life. Of course rescuing her offspring wasn't what they needed. It took years of therapy to realize that she was lovable and loving, and that these qualities hold far more value to her family and others.

As her shame and trauma healing progressed, she came to see that she wasn't loving by giving money, things and time. Gradually she realized that telling them the truth, responding to their actual needs in ways that felt good to her, and setting clear boundaries was really loving them. These days she is becoming clear about the difference between rescue and meeting real needs, but occasionally becomes angry when her children imply that she isn't caring when she says, No.

Lisa's rescue behaviors helped her feel like a good person because her mother and grandmother gave her that reflection only when she served them. Other people make up their identity as caring and giving, and then feel good when their rescuing is received. They get to actually feel good when rescuing, while Lisa was barely able to offset intense shame.

Rescue by Not Telling the Whole Truth

When we hold back information because we don't want to hurt someone's feelings, we are usually operating on conditioning from childhood and the culture. Considering another person's reactions may meet real requirements, but deciding that the other person can't handle the situation when he or she really can, is shaming.

Rescue is a stance that some people like to take. Sometimes a rescuer needs to rescue even when the other person isn't inviting it. For example, the man at the Mexican restaurant who assured me it was okay that I had spilled salsa, and that he would clean it up, thought he was taking care of my shame. But I had no shame. He couldn't see that because he enjoyed being a rescuer. I could see what he was doing, and so I didn't feel shame. Before I understood this behavior, I would have been defensive, wanting to tell him to just clean it up, don't ingratiate himself like that. Since defensiveness is a reaction to shame, I knew that this is what I was feeling. It came from not being perceived accurately. He didn't know that I was capable of spilling salsa and not feeling apologetic about it. My reaction makes sense when I think about the *baby's need to be seen correctly in order to experience belonging in community.* Now that I can observe what is going on, I can avoid wasting my time with shame and the defense against it.

*Any time a person is in a rescuer stance,
he is shaming others.*

This is because he is implying that you can't manage something yourself, that you are too weak or poor or helpless or shame-ridden.

I have found that learning to recognize when others are rescuing, and when they are responding to genuine needs, has been difficult. With so many people out of touch with what is real and what is false, it is confusing to try to differentiate. Again, gathering with others who are studying shame can make it easier. Such a group can watch popular programs together. Stopping every five minutes to discuss what they saw can help educate themselves about each point in the triangle. Television and movies are full of rescue, along with real need-meeting. Rescue can be examined in relation to characters in victim or abuser positions.

Subtle Shame

Facial expressions can communicate a great deal. By the way, Botox inhibits facial expression so that people may not convey shaming in the same way. I had two clients who shamed their husbands, but their faces didn't match their words. Both spoke in soft, expressionless voices, so only the words—and energy—communicated.

Even *shaming that is strikingly obvious is invisible until denial is lifted off.* Facial and body expressions carry shame. Some people present shame on their faces or look embarrassed as a way of life in order to prevent others from delivering more.

On a website was an image of a man with a smile that was more of a grimace, his mouth held tightly. Asking myself how I would respond if he were in front of me, I would say I'd tend to smile reassuringly and let him know that I won't hurt him and not to worry. My rescue patterns are still sufficiently active that his facial request to not shame him works even on me, someone who has studied these communications for a long time.

I know a man who exhibits a shameful expression, makes hesitant sounds and what seem to be uncomfortable body movements. He talks about how he is valued for his business acumen and how he can figure things out. The communication is clear. He wants others to tell him how good, smart, clever, helpful he is, so that he can feel good about himself. If you encountered such a person, wouldn't you want to help him offset his shame?

Looking at pictures in magazines can help in learning to recognize shaming. While I wrote books on sexuality, I collected pictures of people looking sexy in ways the culture defines as not sexual. One picture showed a woman broadcasting sexual energy while holding a young boy against her breast. He looks stricken, yet this picture was used in full-page, glossy magazine ads.

Pictures on magazine covers on newsstands and in grocery stores reveal shaming. After studying *Cosmopolitan* covers for months I could see that the model's typical expression was shaming! Sexual shaming. Women are invited to join the model in putting men down.

Other glamour pictures portray helpless women, hoping you will find them attractive. These are the typical object of sex addicts who know which women cannot say no.

I find it easier to view what expressions communicate in pictures because they are still and constant. I'm not distracted by movement and voice. Around people I am more in tune with energetic communication.

I invite clients to bring in family pictures so I can point out expressions. Given only one picture, I can't be sure if what I see is characteristic, but with three or four, we can assume that this is the way this person typically feels.

Noticing the expressions of strangers may be easier than discovering those of people you know—in particular, your family. Getting together with co-healers and examining each other's pictures can offer useful education.

Humor

Humor can be really effective in stopping the feeling of shame. It can also communicate to others that you already feel shame, and so they don't need to shame you.

After playing racquetball, my partner and I were sitting outside the court when two men went in to play. After a minute they came out and asked us about the rules because they hadn't played for twenty years or more. As they asked, they laughed! What could have just been questions and answers became laughing at themselves for having to ask. We laughed along with them, tacitly agreeing that this was indeed shameful, but we would make light of it.

I found it intriguing that when we ran into each other over the weeks, we all greeted each other warmly as if we had a bond from that exchange. The humor meant we had shared something special.

Once I was aware that I used humor to diminish shame, it became a wonderful signal! When I hear my laugh, I stop myself, say that was shame, and speak again in a straightforward manner. Not only do I stop avoiding shame, I obtain a rapid education as to what I have shame about. For example, when I laughed over not having mowed my lawn, which was getting shaggy, I stopped myself. Yes, I let the grass get long. That's a fact. It is not a cause for embarrassment. It isn't a reason to communicate, Aren't-I-bad, inviting my guest to assure me that she doesn't care.

After many of these examinations, I started naming what would have been self-shaming. When I didn't sweep the cat hair off the floor, I told my friend that the old rules said I should have, or else gave a humor-based apology. I said that it wasn't time for me to want the floor swept based on my own cat hair limits, but if she had a need for my house to be cleaner, I would be glad to do that—for her. This was about facts, not about rules for homes and for shame about them. If a visitor is uncomfortable with clutter or cat hair, I will take care of it. But not because of shame!

In telling stories of failure we can use humor to offset shame. Self-deprecating humor is a way to become congruent with the shame for a time in order to not feel it. The advice to laugh at yourself is really about avoiding shame. The statement that you shouldn't take yourself so seriously is telling you to stop exhibiting shame.

Poor Boundaries

When your employees, friends and relatives have difficulty naming what is acceptable to them, they may feel like blaming you for not knowing. This is a form of shaming. They are likely to tell you that you should have known, or been considerate, or not make them say no. Even if they take responsibility, just their cautious reaction to you conveys that you are causing them problems. If you are seen as a problem causer, you are seen as shame-worthy!

The boss tells the assistant that he wants her to find a caterer for a large meeting he is having over lunch. He explains that he wants nice plates and servingware, not wrapped sandwiches. She has never dealt with caterers, and doesn't know how to find one, particularly a good one. She stands there with a concerned look on her face, but can't tell him what she thinks. Inside she is saying this isn't in her job description, he should do it himself, he should find someone else to do it, why does he have a formal lunch meeting anyway? He should just take them all out to a nice restaurant. She sees herself as one down, he is one up. From this stance she can only view him as a demanding boss.

He can tell that she is shaming him, but doesn't know why. He reacts by giving her more detailed instructions. He wants to fire her. He doesn't like having an employee who acts as if he is abusing her.

If she were able to tell him that she knows nothing about this, then he could either instruct her or find an alternative. They would be equals. They could work it out together.

Because we live in a hierarchic world, this kind of scene is a common source of invisible shaming. Students obey teachers, and resent them for it.

Resentment is shaming.

The women's movement is increasing equality between the sexes, but women give too much power to husbands, and then resent them for it. It only becomes easy to set limits and have boundaries when there is no hierarchy.

Shaming and Boundaries

As you set out to observe what is going on all around us, it might help to study boundaries as a task all its own. Mental health authors have written about the need for boundaries in order to have good relationships and powerful lives, as have writers about shame. This isn't just a problem of the more seriously disturbed person—it is something that all of us confront. Shame brings many to fear having boundaries, because they don't feel deserving. Others over-set boundaries, and use control to get what they want. Few have so little shame that comfortably doing what is right, and communicating it, is easy. These are people who have probably done some healing.

Lying is an easy indicator of lack of boundary-setting. The popular TV show, Frasier, used lying as a common disrupter. Family members were unable to tell each other what they wanted or were doing to avoid being shamed, and so lied about it. Of course, by the end of the show they had been caught or confessed. When joining with your co-healers to study shame, notice lying. This is easiest perhaps when watching TV or movies, and discussing them. It can be fruitful to tell each other your stories of growing up with adults lying, and how you lied because boundaries weren't respected. For example, children say they didn't do something in order to avoid being beaten. And you can tell how you continued to lie even when you no longer needed to.

If you can set aside shame for lying,
then you get to begin learning
why you felt the need to use it to set boundaries.

Most of my male clients have wives who shamed them, and because they didn't realize it wasn't appropriate, they took it. But they hated taking it, so many made the wife pay by having sex outside the marriage and lying. Then they felt worse about themselves, and believed the shaming was appropriate. And around and around. These men didn't believe they had the right to set boundaries regarding how they were treated, and they weren't able to watch someone shame them without absorbing it.

One way to learn about this is to watch couples interact. In restaurants and coffee shops listen to their voices. Notice reactions to subtle shaming. Does the recipient shame back, become controlling, become silent? Over time, notice how common these kinds of exchanges are among those you know.

Defensiveness

Chapter 7, Shaming in Self Defense, addresses the defensive response to shaming. I am including it here, too, because I think it vitally important to understand in healing shame. This response is the most culturally approved and culturally blind. When observing a friend being shamed, one often defensively joins in. That other person is wrong wrong wrong! Without coming to recognize when we ourselves or those we are with are feeling defensive, we are hampered in healing.

Becoming defensive is a guaranteed signal that
shame is being felt.

The circular arguments of couples, where they shame each other around and around, are examples of defensive response to the other, followed by attack. *I didn't do it, it wasn't my fault, you did something worse, you never approve of me, who do you think you are, why do you always treat me like this?*

Members of our culture are so shame-laden that shame is triggered even by healthy anger and constructive criticism. Even more comes from unhealthy anger and unconstructive criticism. People dance around each other as they try to not feel shame, or get the other person to take it back, or somehow make it not happen. It is sadly uncommon for a person to be able to hear shaming directed at oneself and calmly observe.

Defensiveness is always a reaction to
the experience of shame.

Disagreement, explaining why a comment is incorrect, and saying that this kind of treatment needs to stop can be done with no shaming. Without shame it is possible to assess and respond with no emotion. With shame, the first reaction is to defend oneself.

Studying Defensiveness

It might help to know that every single person gets defensive! It seems like a normal human reaction.

You feel it. Notice the physical sensation of stomach tightening, of anger, of questioning how this could be happening. Defensiveness is a very unpleasant feeling because it is really shame. It is the attempt to defend against the emotion of shame by proving that it isn't appropriate to feel. The truth is, Yes it isn't appropriate to feel toxic shame! But the person well trained with shame can't believe that, and struggles to be right, to be not harmful, to be not stupid.

Although studying one's own defensiveness is a long-term project, it can be quite simple to begin noticing it in others! It goes on everywhere, as shaming does. When I ask the person bagging my groceries to put them in fewer bags, I am often met with defensiveness, as if I were saying he is doing it wrong. Observing people at coffee shops can reveal how many feel mildly defensive over having to give their order. I wonder if they fear they aren't doing it right, or worry that any hesitation or awkwardness will be a bother.

Defensiveness can be seen in one's posture, and in a pulling in of energy, a holding back, a hesitation. Frowns and puzzled expressions are noticeable.

Movies and TV are full of hatred carried to the extreme of violence. Instead of joining the characters in justifying their hatred, step back and *examine why they feel it*. What does it do for them? What would they feel if they didn't feel hate? How would they have handled the situation differently? How much of the hate was directed into the desire for revenge? How much pleasure do you receive from joining them in revenge? How are the writers and directors and actors trying to get us to feel hatred and revenge in order to avoid shame? How do they set out to intensify emotions when bringing a group of people together? Movies in a theater are almost guaranteed to take us out of our ordinary, shame-filled lives and give us a break by having made-up feelings—for a while.

While it is easier to examine the purpose of the writers and directors with a remote that can stop the film, going with co-healers to a theater and talking afterward can provide information, too. Each person can relate the experience of being out of the normal world for a couple of hours. How does it change your physical sensation of being in your body? How is your stress level?

Chapter 6
Ordinary, Everyday Shaming

I believe a separate chapter is necessary for the kind of shaming that is most difficult to observe. This is the kind where someone points to the wall, says, Isn't that an amazing picture, look at the complex use of colors! and all you see is a painted wall. There is nothing there! This is not an exaggeration. I point out shaming to clients, to friends, and occasionally strangers, and get this reaction. They shake their heads, their faces looking puzzled. I can hear the voice in their heads saying, "What are you talking about?" A year or so later these same people smile when a new member of group has the same reaction, now that he or she can see the full color image.

During talks I gave, I got to see how difficult it is for people to recognize everyday shaming when I offered an example from my own life: In the hospital I had told a nutritionist that I don't eat sugar, and need meals that don't include it. I explained that I eat high-protein meals with healthy fats and low carbs. I even explained that my hypoglycemia requires that. But she argued with me, holding a container of pudding in her hand! I finally said she needed to come back when I wasn't right out of surgery and under the influence of drugs. She held up the container and said, "But what about the pudding?" Isn't this amazing? Then the next day she came back and tried to talk me into eating ice cream!

As I presented this information to my audience, I smiled and shook my head.

I explained that I enjoyed telling this story in shaming tones, as it was an example of a time during which I still felt like shaming. Then I presented it in factual tones. I said that she apparently had some investment in patients eating sweets, and had issues that brought her to argue with a patient who was very clear about her needs. I wonder if she is burned out, or her brain isn't working well. I said this with no shaming tone. I truly wondered about her decisions.

Of interest is that audiences do not perceive that I am shaming, even when I say I am and present the non-shaming alternative. Complaining about incomprehensible behavior is so accepted as normal and appropriate that only the rare person knew that I was shaming. This example has made it really clear that healing has to start with learning what ordinary shaming looks like. Without this study, my audiences would not see or understand that the attitude directed at them is harmful. Each of us needs to know that when we feel defensive, or are uncomfortable with the tone directed at us, we may very well be the object of shaming. This is why watching movies, TV, and ads in a group is useful. Stopping the DVR or DVD every three minutes to check for the presence of shaming will gradually reveal the ordinary variety. One or two of the group will see various kinds and gradually educate each other.

Audiences didn't know I was shaming when talking about the nutritionist because we are blinded to perceiving shaming when it is incorporated into gossip. Take another look at the same situation, now from the nutritionist's point of view. What if she were in the audience, knowing I was talking about her? Then would everyone see the picture?

What if you were the nutritionist and I said my subtly shaming comments directly to you. Would you know that I was shaming, then? What if I had laughed, and said, "You wanted to know about the pudding even after I told you several times that I don't eat sugar!" Then adding, "You aren't hearing that I have boundaries here, and you aren't listening. And on top of that, what school did you go to that says sugar is good for hospital patients? Or anyone? Whoever said that ice cream is good for you? Everyone knows that it tastes good and that is the absolutely only reason for eating it."

Perhaps it can be seen as shaming if you put yourself in her shoes. No one likes to receive it even while we don't think it is shaming if we are delivering it.

Of course this nutritionist would have felt bad even if I had delivered my message firmly with no criticism. If I had told her that I wasn't going to discuss it, if I told her that she was to stop arguing with me and just do what I say. If I said that I was going to ask for a conversation with her superior because I want to understand why a hospital employee argues with me about something that has nothing to do with my needs or my reason for being in the hospital.

This would have been setting good boundaries without having to attack her. In this culture loaded with defensiveness and fear of feeling wronged or being seen as a bad person, people are just as likely to get a bad reaction to boundary-setting as they are to shaming someone. Actually, shaming can usually be better tolerated because we are prepared for it! We can respond with our well rehearsed defensive style, angrily attack back, and refuse to perceive the boundary.

Learning to See Acculturated Shaming

As I started to write this chapter, I wondered how it would be possible to describe a form of shaming that can't be seen because it is so concealed in the culture. I want to play DVDs with examples. Even then it might be difficult to recognize until observing long enough.

I'm going to provide statements I overheard from people in restaurants and malls, then re-state them with stronger words with the same message, and finally, re-state them without shaming.

Here's the first one. A woman came in the swinging door of the health food store with two small children. One child opened the door onto my cart, and the second rolled the mat up as she scuffed her feet over it. The mother looked at me apologetically and told them with annoyance that they were accidents waiting to happen.

Perhaps others would see this as critical, too, but still, it is also seen as entirely appropriate parenting, as if parents should complain about their children. I thought so when I was the parent of a young child.

If would be easier to see if she said, "Get back, you idiot! And you, watch where you put your stupid feet! Whoever gave you the right to live in this world?"

What if she didn't shame? She might have reached out and grabbed the hand of each child, holding them outside the door until she saw that it was clear. She wouldn't have held them responsible for perceiving something they are too young to see. She knew that when they were two, they needed to have a hand held or be in a stroller. She doesn't understand what kind of restraint they need when they are a little older. She blames them for this.

Another example: The teenager came into the restaurant with her family, and as they walked to their table, she said, "I want to call Josh." Sounds innocent enough, but her tone communicated, "Why do I have to be here with you freaks, anyway, I so don't want to be here. You never let me do what I want." Can you imagine the tone? See why it's hard to communicate this in writing?

If she were to have a boundary so that she wasn't left with shaming as the only expression possible, she might have told her parents that she was going to the parking lot to call Josh, and here's what to order, tell me when it's here. If the parents wanted a nice family dinner, they won't get to have her included. But she wouldn't have joined them anyway, so why not allow the boundary?

Through the window I watched a couple on the patio at Starbucks. They weren't speaking, but shame was flowing. The woman flipped her foot up and down and had a slight frown. If she had been by herself I would have wondered what was wrong. Since she was sitting opposite a man who was leaning forward with his head down, I didn't have to wonder. She was finding great fault with him, and he felt as if he deserved it. Their bodies said it all.

If she were to speak, she might have said, "Whatever possessed me to be married to you? I just can't believe that you have done this, and then hidden it from me. What were you possibly thinking?" I don't even have to know what he did wrong. It isn't the issue.

He has nothing to say. He is bad. He can't even defend himself by shaming back, by being defensive, by explaining it away. He has given up.

If she had been speaking clearly I would have expected something like, "I'm upset about what you did. I'm also upset that you felt the need to hide it from me. I have a lot of thinking to do about this, I'm not sure what it means about trusting you." She would have looked right at him and spoken with no criticism, just concern and feelings.

He would have responded with grief instead of toxic shame. Actually, he would respond with shame, as apparently he did something hurtful. But then grief would follow because he knows that he has done something that can't be undone. He has to regain her trust.

My many clients who shamed their husbands were unable to have healthy anger and resorted to a quality of powerless hurt. Even if they said they weren't shaming, when someone communicates that they have been hurt, shame arrives. With the couple above, the man had done something to feel shame about. In most of my clients' situations, this is also true. I work with sex addicts, and most have violated their marriage bond. But after they reveal everything, go to 12-step meetings in order to stop, and have started a course of therapy, their wives usually still have difficulty. This is because they can't access healthy anger that is needed to accomplish grief (see Chapter 17 for information on the essential qualities of grief). If they can't grieve, they can't release the past and engage in the new truth of the present.

I counsel the husbands to set boundaries around how much blame and hurt they will tolerate.

No Shame on You

Our workshops, called No Shame on You, focus on ordinary, everyday shaming. We use skits to demonstrate the difference between the *communication of shame* and the *delivery of information*. The very same words can convey valuable information to a spouse, or communicate that the spouse is wrong and stupid and had better change. We emphasize that *healing shame doesn't mean deciding to stop!* Better to keep right on taking it in, but for now, observing it. When we make ourselves stop doing something, we lose the available education that will automatically lead to healing. *Observing brings education.*

It is understood that children who are physically and emotionally and sexually abused will internalize shame. They will have psychological, social and medical outcomes. Psychotherapy for trauma has evolved in order to assist in grieving away the experiences, which includes removing the shame. Books have been written for people who want to heal the kind of shame that is woven into their very identity. Now we can all heal from the ordinary, everyday shaming going on all around us.

In order to change the *world's* human relating, we need to address *acculturated shame*. Shaming that is integrated into the culture is not easily seen. Healing begins with recognizing the mild, everyday forms. Then, we can stop this shame from coming in. Next, we can learn how to stop shaming others.

It is difficult to describe acculturated shaming because it is accepted as normal. It often takes time for couples to see how they shame each other.

Voice Tone

Tone of voice communicates as much as words. A couple sits in my office. The wife tells us how she doesn't know if she wants to continue the marriage because he flirts, and when angry, calls her names. Name-calling is obvious shaming, as it is telling people they are defective. Both the husband and the wife could see this. However, neither could recognize that she was shaming him with her tone. She had a mildly hurt, how-could-you-do-this-to-me tone. He reacted with defensiveness. When I pointed out her tone, she argued with me. I asked her to notice how her voice was coming from her throat, not from down in her chest. When she could speak from a deeply felt, empowered place, she was able to give him the same information about what felt bad to her, but without shaming him. He was still defensive, but less so.

When feeling like a victim (different from being truly victimized), people will present their experience in a shaming manner whether the subject is government, the banking system, other drivers, spouses, family members, children, politicians, or anyone who is believed to be doing something wrong. A non-shaming response is forward-moving, information-stating, with the voice coming from the chest. There is no head-shaking! No implication of, "How could they do this!"

Gossip is a form of joining with others to shame those who are bad, stupid, thoughtless, too wealthy, too fat, too anything not approved of.

When an investment partner and I had to foreclose on a property, we expressed victimized shock at the owner's ongoing lies and manipulations accompanied by tears and regret. After I pulled us out of this reaction, we were able to see that the owner was willing to violate his integrity to try to retain the property, and we could comfortably stand our ground. Not having to feel shame for causing his distress, we didn't have to shame him for his manipulations. When we stopped shaming him, we stopped wasting time and energy. We could clearly see what was called for.

When one client laughs too loudly, or says something "inappropriate," his wife gives him a look, or makes a sound, or says his name. She is shaming him in a culturally accepted manner. Others in the room may join her with chuckles and smiles and nods. Whenever people are out of touch and do odd things, others are allowed to shame them. Then everyone lives in fear of doing odd things and being shamed for it!

I sat at dinner while my friend shamed her husband with no words. She didn't even look at him shamingly. Her energy was hardened, and she appeared separate from him even though they sat only a few inches apart. She didn't know her anger was shaming him. He responded defensively, but didn't know that her manner of addressing what he had done was not healthy. I described the scene, and they could both grasp it, although it took time to change their behavior.

A man who applied for a line of credit told me how he won when his bank had at the last minute required proof of income. He wanted and got an explanation, but when it didn't suit him, he cancelled his application. His tone said he had gotten one over on them. He relieved his own shame by shaming them, even though he hadn't gotten his credit line. When I pointed this out, with no shaming, another man overhearing, said, "Showed them!" He wanted to triangulate with me against the man, but with humor so the man wouldn't be offended. It's possible that his entire purpose was to invoke humor to offset the man's shame.

Women's acculturated shaming is more difficult to see than men's because women are the good gender. We are entitled to shame men for being boorish pigs, too interested in themselves, not adequately meeting our needs. Men's shame is easier to see because men are the bad gender. When they shame others it is seen as bad. They more overtly call names and tell women what is wrong with them. Of course they pay for it because invisible shaming is received in return. Even when women name-call, it is not perceived to be as harmful as when men do it—because men are seen as deserving it! Both genders shame equally, and the shaming of both genders is equally harmful!

Watch. Listen. Notice. Feel. Sigh. Breathe. Talk.

My job is getting shaming spouses to change how they speak to their partner. I worked with one woman on how she said, "I don't like that," to her husband. When she held herself back, she looked at him sideways, her soft voice communicating that he was really bad for doing something she didn't like. When she was able to fully claim her dislike for what he did, and say it straight out, looking him in the eyes, she was merely expressing what she felt, what was going on inside of her. There was *no shaming*, just *facts*.

We don't see the acculturated shame going on
all around us all the time.

When Kathie Lee Gifford made fun of Larry King on national television for everything he said, including not remembering what was in his autobiography, it was seen by her and the audience as funny. You are supposed to be a good sport when shame is delivered as humor. He would be seen as a wimp for telling her to stop.

Critical, condescending humor is considered entertaining,
bonding and witty. It is shaming.

When Larry King was on *The View*, Barbara Walters shamingly peppered him with the question, Why didn't he search for his son, Larry King, Jr., until the son was 30? She did this to invite the audience to triangulate with her against Larry. Then she pulled out of it by complimenting him for putting this information in his autobiography. She abused him, and then rescued him from her abuse. This is typical of her interview style. Why does this make her popular? Do women enjoy watching another woman shame men? Is it seeing someone shame celebrities and powerful people? Or is it enjoying the shaming of anyone?

Why is a yawning cat the cutest thing ever but people are suppose to hide their own yawning?

Notice how many TV ads shame one of the actors, and indirectly, shame you for not buying something. Or how women are invited to shame men for not understanding why this item is best.

Embarrassment

Many people say they don't feel shame, they're just embarrassed, or uncomfortable. Shame is on a continuum from mild discomfort to intensely hideous emotional pain. Embarrassment and discomfort are at the milder end—and are less likely to be seen as shame. As we educate ourselves about this everyday variety, we can see how often we and others receive and deliver it. A sure signal is the feeling of defensiveness—any need to claim that we aren't shame-worthy or shame-deserving. Studying defensiveness might be easier than identifying shame, as it is not so hidden. Notice when you hold back, or have a slight frown as you try to prove what you believe is true. More intense defensiveness, of course, includes counter-attack, loudness, refusing to listen, and the classic circular arguments where both people defend. Study the *ordinary, everyday defensiveness*, though. This can be educational. When you say, "How can you think that?" or "Why did you say that?" notice if there is protest in the voice or if it is a true, straight-out question.

Rudeness

Countless clients have looked at me seriously as they ask, "But isn't that rude?" Or they say, "I don't want to be rude."

Rude is a shame word. It can be replaced by a description of the behavior and a boundary. "When you keep pushing me along, it makes me uncomfortable and I want you to stop." "You keep interrupting me and I'd like to finish what I was saying." The behaviors are addressed with boundaries. Calling them rude merely shames the person and does not create a boundary. It leaves the name-caller powerless, expecting the other person to feel shame and then figure out what is needed to make you happy.

Classic Ordinary Shame Sentences

How often do you hear words such as thoughtless, selfish, rude, inconsiderate, unkind, stupid, crazy, negative, dumb, liar, and cheater? Let us hope not often directed at you! These words are integrated into our language, and only seen as shaming if they are spoken in a harsh, shaming tone. "You are such an idiot!!" We all agree that's shaming. But what if someone says in a normal tone, "Honey, that wasn't very thoughtful, was it? What do you think you might have done instead?" Or, with humor, "Oh my god, I was so stupid, what was I thinking?" Or a friend acts embarrassed at not having vacuumed, which implies that you are criticizing her for it. She reacts as if you have shamed her, when the shame is internally generated. But you have to say, No problem, I don't mind, in order to relieve her shame and to make it clear that you aren't shaming her.

Suspiciousness

Suspicious tones are shaming. Non-shaming would be asking directly for information and receiving the answer. The woman at the customer service counter, who was required to leave her package before entering the store, said, "What are you going to do with it?" This question could have been a clear request for information, but her suspicious tone said the employee was sure to lose it or steal it. She was expressing shaming anger that had nothing to do with the woman behind the counter.

Impatience

Impatience is shaming. It implies that the person it's directed at is doing something wrong or too slowly. Being impatient when children "dawdle," a shaming word, tells them that they are misbehaving. In truth, the child has no internal programming to alert him that timing is important and is only cooperating because it is required. If this is understood, then the parent could set up a reward system for the child for doing something that to him has no meaning. This reward brings some external meaning. Shaming a child for not being obedient doesn't support cooperation.

Impatience is depended on by people who have difficulty setting boundaries. One wife talked about playing the waiting game as she criticized her husband to other wives. He never left on time for social events or church services. It wasn't within her perception of herself and her marriage to take her own car and leave on time. If she understands that she is shaming her husband and engendering his unexpressed anger, she can practice developing new boundaries in order not to use shame.

Defensiveness

Defensiveness is always a sign that someone is feeling shame and wants to turn it on the other person. I keep repeating this because *defensiveness is such a vital response to understand when learning about shame*. We all feel shame. We all feel defensive. Everyone around us feels shame. Everyone around us will be defensive.

When a boss tells an employee that the performance isn't up to standard, his employee may defensively argue, explain why he didn't do well, or claim that he is doing fine. The tone indicates whether this is presented as information or is accompanied by a defensive attitude—a shame-based desire to make the evaluation untrue. The boss may have spoken with a put-down shaming tone, or he may have just given information. Either way, most people will feel shame for not being viewed as adequate. The person who can't argue with the boss might tell friends or a mate how unfair or wrong the boss was. Or he might believe the boss is right, and feel the shame full-out.

Defensiveness goes on all around us. A customer asks why the store no longer carries a brand of cat food, and the manager makes a case for why that brand shouldn't be carried. When the nutritionist argued with me about sugar, she shook her head as if I were attacking her personally for wanting me to eat ice cream. When I called my phone company's advertising section to ask why I was being billed for a service I had cancelled, the woman's tone defensively implied that I was not very bright because I couldn't take her word for the charges.

Anytime someone thinks they haven't done something in accordance with social values and rules and requirements, getting poor grades or making mistakes or providing poor parenting or thousands of other possibilities, defensiveness is a likely reaction to ward off shame.

Accepting Shaming

Shaming is so integrated into the culture that people find it easier to be shamed than told a painful truth. A friend showed up for our meeting really late. What if I shamed him by saying, "God, that was really thoughtless, how could you think I should just wait around for you?" He could have said he was sorry, or defensively explained that it was on account of traffic and his phone died, or told me I'm too demanding. But if I looked him in the eye and spoke in a straightforward, honest voice with no shaming to tell him that I don't like what he did, he has no culturally approved way to cope with it. He would feel toxic shame. If he is healing shame, he can feel healthy shame, explore his motives, and acknowledge them to me. This will enhance his shame-healing and his intimacy with me.

Criticism

Criticizing table manners or driving, telling someone in a whiny tone that they're doing something wrong, treating others as if they don't have the same rights are among the most common forms of shaming. There is non-shaming criticism, too, of course, what has been called constructive criticism. But even constructive criticism can still be delivered with a shaming tone. Bosses need to convey information after a job isn't done correctly, or could be done more efficiently. This is constructive and appropriate. However, if the tone implies that the employee should have already known, or the boss is superior, or if the words are impatiently delivered, then shame is interwoven with the information. Only the delivery needs to change.

Because criticism is usually perceived as shaming, it is hard for most people to deliver it. Working with newer clients, I remain aware of how they may receive the useful information I offer. Even knowing I'm not shaming, they can very well feel shame anyway. Any feedback about what we are doing that isn't good for us or for others, or that is far from perfect, is considered shameful in this culture. Over time my clients come to appreciate that my information is useful and are able to receive it without feeling shamed.

One of my co-healers gave examples of how she shames her husband. She mentioned his wrinkled pants, the choice of shirt when he is meeting with wealthy clients, and how he freezes up when she feels isolated from him. His shame prevents him from having boundaries with her. He can't say, "These wrinkles are acceptable to me. These clients are more interested in what I can do for them than in my shirt. Don't criticize me."

A client gave me two recent examples from his life that he can now see are shaming, when before he would have questioned himself. At a renowned zoo he showed his tickets, wondering aloud if he needed a different kind. The woman shoved them back at him, saying "Can't you read?" with disgust. He didn't know that he had a kind of ticket that qualified for any exhibit.

The second instance took place at his bank, where he went to ask why a deposit hadn't been recorded on his line of credit. The banker explained that he had put it in the wrong account. She handed the paperwork back to him, and said, "Mr. D., you should have known!"

Now that he knows this is shaming, he can let it slide on by. When he didn't have that objectivity, he felt shame! Every one of us has to learn to see shaming that is woven into the culture, refuse to take it in, and heal our own.

This client carries a great load of shame beginning with having been unloved as a child, shamed throughout childhood because of being odd and not fitting in, and then from being alcoholic and having extra-marital affairs, which created his own shame. In spite of all of this he is learning to see shaming, to refuse to take it in even from his wife, and gradually stop his angry response to it. Observing all around us, including our family members, allows the internalized shaming to become clear, to be seen as outside the self, and to understand that it can be healed.

Competition

Competing with the implication that winning makes one better than the losers shames everyone. Team sports, even at the elementary school level, provoke shaming from parents, classmates and spectators. Even the winners feel shame because they know they could be and have been the losers. Needing to win in order to avoid the bad feeling leaves one vulnerable for the next time. People who have been very successful in their careers can feel devastation when unable to continue or after retirement. One reason is that they can no longer win.

Everyday Shaming

Do you know how it feels when someone pushes past you in a store, implying that you were in the way? Or a driver honks because you were in the wrong lane or cut him off? How does it feel when the teller asks how you are without looking at you, and you know she doesn't care? These are examples of everyday shaming.

The boss frowns at you when you are three minutes late to a meeting. A co-worker thinks she is doing more than her share and shuns you in the lounge. An employee treats you like the father who abused her—she's afraid of you and walking on egg shells. The woman standing in the bank line glares at everyone.

A common shaming from parents and others is to ask, "What makes you think you could do that?" When I was writing my fifth book in a park, a man asked me what I was doing, then proceeded to tell me that it's not easy to write a book and get it published; what made me think I could? I thought he was strange, but didn't realize that he enjoyed shaming others and I was handy. He failed because I told him I had a publisher and had already published books. I felt victorious as I put him in his place. Now I see that he was medicating his shame by perceiving me as a stupid woman who thought she could do something done by few. I didn't win anything. I merely prevented him from diminishing his shame. He had to find another alternative.

Even harsher shaming is the question, "What makes you think you deserve that?" When a friend was in high school, her troop won a competition that entitled it to a free trip to Japan. She was excited until her mother asked her that question. Her mother's own miserable life had made her jealous of her daughter, and so she took the edge off her pleasure by making her clean tile grout with a toothbrush in order to earn the necessary pocket money. While this is seen as mean by the culture, it is harder to see that the daughter would experience this as communication of her lack of worth. When a mother doesn't feel loving and delighted for her daughter's success, the girl can take it to mean there is something wrong with her, even while she and her friends will say it's the mother who is bad.

Managing the Emotions of Others

When people are cautious and reluctant and hesitant, they can elicit feelings of shame. You are being seen as someone people need to be reluctant and hesitant around.

Acting hesitant communicates that the other person is dangerous and has to be managed. When my co-healer was reluctant and apologetic, I got annoyed. As we processed, I saw that I took on shame when people acted as if I could hurt them, and as if they had to be careful around me. Then I realized that it was just her fear from having to manage both of her parents to avoid emotional abuse. She had projected it onto me—and everyone around her. I had to understand this in order to not take on shame.

If you think back on conversations in which the other person was hesitant to tell you what they were going to do, or about an experience they had, what did you feel? You might not have felt shame because your methods to avoid it were engaged. My own reaction was anger. I was objecting to the implication that I was dangerous and the other person had to handle me to keep me from reacting in bad ways.

More generally, *when people are afraid of you they are shaming you*—unless you are someone to be afraid of, of course.

An example of invisible shaming occurred when a co-healer's husband talked with an acquaintance. The acquaintance asked him questions about still being at the same job, the tone implying that he had not bettered himself. The husband responded defensively, a signal that he was being shamed, and felt shame. In order to not feel shame, he needed to see that he was being shamed. This is a good example of why learning to see is so valuable in the process of refusing to take shame on.

Do you manage the emotions of others? This can be in the form of holding back information so the other person doesn't become angry, shame-filled, abandoning, or shaming. What do you do to manage those potential reactions? You may smile, or use an affectionate tone of voice, or change the subject to something neutral.

Notice why you might want to do that. Perhaps it's to avoid having the other person feel the shame you expect if you were to be right out there with your comments.

Pretty much everyone apologizes for actions that don't warrant apologizing, in order to reduce shame. Common examples are: not remembering or misunderstanding something someone said, forgetting someone's name, not hearing correctly, not knowing the answer to a question, walking too fast or too slowly, wearing the wrong clothes, choosing the wrong movie or restaurant or gift.

Forgetting what someone said or their name is seen as not valuing that person. It isn't. Many of us have poor memories. I am one. Not only can I not remember names, I can't remember faces. A co-investor and I met very many people over the course of our business. He remembered them all, I remembered few. He soon learned to tell me who the person was, and then I explained that I have poor visual memory. I felt no shame about this, and in time he lost his own at pointing this out in front of the person. He helped me avoid having the person feel slighted or making other interpretations of my not responding to them. He helped me present the truth.

If you know it is your memory, and that you are not slighting someone, then there is no reason for shame—healthy or toxic. Instead of saying I'm sorry, I explain that it's my memory. This is the truth.

Isn't it odd that we feel shame when not understanding what someone said? If neither the speaker nor listener has shame, then it quickly becomes obvious that communication hasn't occurred. Facial expressions register confusion. Then one person can say, I don't think I heard you correctly, or the other says, I don't think you heard me correctly. Then they go back and do it again. Shame comes when the listener thinks he must hear correctly. Then the speaker feels as if she has to make sure the listener doesn't feel shame. Or, she shames him for not understanding.

Then there are the really ordinary areas of shame agreed upon by all. You are shame-worthy if you have underarm sweat (unless you just worked out), stains, wrinkles or cat hair on clothing, smelly gas, skin wrinkles, fat, inadequate social skills, lack of sex appeal, if you are drunk, going to work late, breaking engagements at the last minute. Perhaps healthy shame is appropriate for some of these, but toxic shame for any will prevent changing. Contrary to popular belief, shame doesn't help us truly change from the inside out. I overheard a young man swimming laps get out of the pool and berate himself for doing poorly. He sounded like his own shaming coach.

The culture agrees that we should feel shame for shaming,
and shame for just having shame.

When discovering the shaming going on all around us all the time, many people start looking at how they shame others. This is true for parents in particular, as harming children, of course, brings guilt and shame. If the shame is too strong, it may interfere with examining it. I really want to counsel everyone to acknowledge that you have shame; you have shamed others; if you are a parent you, of course, have shamed your children.

The first step in healing shame is accepting that
every single one of has shamed others.
We have all been mean.
We have all harmed.
There is no way around this.

If we feel compelled to prove that we haven't harmed anyone, our shame will multiply. I found it a relief to realize that I along with everyone else has harmed. It is unavoidable because of the culture we all grew up in. Shaming was modeled. We were shamed if we didn't shame in the manner our parents did. Then we were shamed for not shaming in the manner our peers did.

Somehow I didn't feel shame for just having it, but most of my clients have. What an incredibly difficult conundrum this one is! If you feel shame just for having shame, it makes it difficult to take a look at your form of shame! This is why working in a group of people who are all healing shame is truly necessary. If you can look around the room at others who feel shame, and know that they shouldn't have to, this knowing has a chance of being reflected back onto you.

When I tell people that very little apology is appropriate, they frequently argue with me. They say they don't want to be rude. When I gave the example of mutual crashing of grocery carts, and laughing together over it with no apology, several audience members believed that apology was needed. A couple couldn't hear that I was talking about mutual crashing, not one person crashing into another. Yet, even then, I don't apologize. I say something like, Oh, I wasn't watching where I was going. Or, I didn't see you around that corner. Or, Oops! This feels appropriate when I haven't intended to hit someone.

The woman at the bank took my deposit with an annoyed expression. Even if she didn't know she was shaming, she was. When done, she smiled and said, Have a nice day, but she was acting. I know this had nothing to do with me. She was broadcasting shame from an internal process. I wasn't affected because I could see it. At the emergency vet's I was the same person, but received three different reactions. The couple with the sick dog wanted to engage me; the receptionist, without saying a word, acted as though I were a bother and should sit down and shut up; and the vet was friendly, business-like and efficient.

When someone is irritated with you they are holding you responsible, which shames you. One cause of annoyance is the inability to set boundaries. A client presented a list of ways in which his wife and daughter treated him like a convenience instead of a person. He felt compelled to let them have their way, and was left with annoyance as the only recourse, expressed with an impatient tone and body language, which were shaming them. We saw that had each situation been handled differently, his family members would have responded favorably. With small and easy-to-set-boundaries, his irritation wouldn't have grown, and he wouldn't have shamed. We did learn that he was projecting his parents onto his wife and daughter, as his only value was what he did for them. In the present, all he had to do was not carry all the bags—just hand them out. Not take a backseat. Instead of pouting, he could have engaged both wife and daughter. When he was unable to perceive his right to boundaries regarding his role in the family, he couldn't do anything but pout and shame them.

Shaming is sometimes called anger. It isn't anger.
It's shaming.
Healthy, discharging anger doesn't shame!

I explain to couples that when they hold anger back, it is likely to come out as shaming. Converting anger into feeling hurt is one way that women typically avoid anger. What isn't seen is that telling someone that they hurt you is a form of shaming. And it doesn't offer a recourse for healing. If someone tells you that she is really angry about what you did, and directs it right at you, she can discharge the anger and grieve it away. A process leading to a conclusion becomes possible. Shaming, on the other hand, goes on and on and won't lead anywhere. Tears without anger won't heal.

On his TV program, Dr. Phil shames his guests, his tone asking how they could possibly think that was acceptable behavior. He invites the audience to triangulate with him against the guests.

Parents shame children with a critical tone even if their words are neutral. They do this with impatience and sighs. Exasperation. The sigh says, You are so bad or uncontrollable that I just give up. This gives the power to the child because the parent is relinquishing it.

Sighs of displeasure are one of the most common ways to express shaming. This kind is so different from the one that expresses satisfaction and understanding and robust delight. This one is hopeless, giving up. Shaming.

Self-Shaming

Even after years of studying shaming and healing my own, I discovered from writing this book and pulling my attention to my own self-shaming, that I had some very obvious kinds! These included apologizing for my poor memory, for erratic lawn mowing and floor sweeping; laughing when saying something that might be hard to hear and laughing at myself for having unhealthy patterns. With my shame level very low, I could confront these remaining forms with amazement and pleasure. I would stop myself and say, "Oh, I'm shaming myself. I'm going to say this again." I got to see what it was like to stop! It took focus on the very ordinary shame—with my co-healers—to stop acculturated self-criticism.

Chapter 7
Shaming in Self Defense

Avoiding Triggering Others' Shame

Everyone hates feeling shame. Many people also hate triggering shame in someone else because of knowing how bad it feels. We also want to avoid that person shaming us for shaming them. This is a major reason people have difficulty setting boundaries. If someone calls for a long talk, and you prefer to finish your project and talk later, you must declare the desire with a sense of apology, communicating that you really want to talk, please don't be mad. You know that if cut off, the caller may feel rejected or unloved, the experience of shame.

Helping Others Avoid Feeling Shame

We as a culture are as eager to prevent others from feeling shame as we are to avoid feeling it ourselves, even if we don't provoke it. We don't want them to feel this kind of pain, and we don't want them to defend themselves from it because it is likely to include shaming or attacking us. We smile, feign interest, don't set limits; act nice, very helpful, agreeable, and use other methods of inhibiting another's experience of shame.

Defending Ourselves

When those who carry shame—all of us—are shamed, the choice is to either accept the shame and feel badly, or defend against it.

Shame-free people aren't defensive
because they don't need to defend themselves
against shame.

Many people are lying in wait for shame to be directed at them. I deliver information without shame almost all the time, but someone who expects to be shamed won't be able to tell the difference. For example, if I tell someone who has been consistently ten minutes late that I would like him to come on time, I am likely to be met with long, defensive explanations about why he was late.

Couples engaging in circular arguments are defending against the partner's defending, round and round.

In my practice I have overheard men respond defensively to everything their wives say. It becomes a lifestyle. While this may avoid the feeling of shame, it creates a victim mentality. The men feel perpetually victimized, and resist. Their shame prevents them from setting boundaries with their wives, or even seeing if the wife is not shaming or holding them responsible for something.

Society supports the belief that men are bad. Women are the good gender, doing no wrong while men are the crude, obnoxious, abusive ones. Men have an easier time getting started in couples therapy because they already think they are bad. I get to help them relieve shame in order to see what they really want to change. Women come in with complaints about others, and because they are defined as good, have more difficulty in seeing how they are harmful. Shame is more painful for women because it has been more completely denied, and then not felt. Women can defend against feeling bad by seeing men as the bad ones. Men agree.

I asked a couple of women if they wanted to come to Friday night racquetball challenge court. One spent five minutes explaining why it wouldn't work for her, three times telling me it wasn't personal. I could see that she has a history of being accused of hurting others when setting boundaries. Now she expects such a reaction. Sadly, she has developed an active approach to defending herself against feeling shame for potentially shaming me. It prevented her from seeing me at all.

How We Shame Others

When we feel shame, we shame others even when we don't want to. It's built into the culture. If we don't shame others, we will stand out as different and not fit in. I am learning how to not shame, but still find myself doing it. The woman who talked compulsively about how it wasn't personal that she didn't want to play racquetball with me brought out my shaming. I didn't say anything, but inside I was thinking, *Really, how stupid to think I would take it personally; listen, just stop jabbering and let me get onto the court.* When I can't set boundaries, such as walking away in mid-sentence, I lapse into shaming.

Defensiveness is a sign of feeling shame. Always. It's that tone and facial expression that say, No, you're wrong, I'm not bad! It includes the victim presentation of: you hurt me, I've been wronged, it isn't fair, they are out to get me. These bad feelings invite the listener to rescue in order to feel like a good person, relieving her own experience of shame for a time.

A client I referred to an addictions treatment program went immediately. When his therapist there called me, she used a shaming tone in describing him, as if he were a difficult person. Even in the midst of my coming to understand that we all shame and receive shaming, I carried a remote fantasy that treatment programs wouldn't do this. After all, these are the very programs that help people heal shame!

I drove through a parking lot where two streets intersect, with only one stop sign. As I approached, the car that was stopped at the stop sign started driving. He obviously thought I had a stop sign, too. I started to get annoyed—shaming him for breaking the rules—when I realized that he didn't know. He made a mistake. If I had grown up in a shame-free community I would never have had to think about it. All of us would understand that no one is perfect, and we would work together to get everyone through the intersection. There would be no need for comments such as, "Hey, get out of my way!" or "Sorry, I didn't see that you had no stop sign," or "That's okay, don't worry about it."

While writing books on sexuality, I was frequently attacked. I gave a workshop at a conference, and afterwards almost all of the participants came up to me to thank me for the way I addressed sexual addiction. However, when I was sent a "representative" sample of attendee evaluations, they were all negative! When shaming felt good, I was enraged and told a lot of others, inviting them to triangulate with me against the leader of the conference—the actual person who didn't like what I said.

Now I can smile, knowing that my subject was highly controversial then, and guess that the conference promoter was a sex addict himself. The world is full of people who were so shamed and harmed in childhood that of course they will see a subject through their distortions. What a waste to become negatively charged and find someone to blame! Really, it's rather entertaining. When members of my professional listserv write madly about discrimination against our understanding of sexuality and healing, I sometimes point out that controversy is really good as it is getting people's attention! I really mean it! What a change for me!

Shaming Spouses to Avoid Shame and Self-Hate

Spouses and children are the easiest scapegoats to use in order to stop that dreadful feeling of self-hate. Many of my clients have discovered that when shame begins to emerge, they are likely to pick a fight with their spouses. They do this by criticizing. One woman would return to the subject of her husband's infidelity and want him to move out. This alternated with loving and appreciating him. When she felt self-hating, nothing would convince her that she didn't truly need him to leave.

Shame is such a terrible feeling that methods to avoid it can be entirely rationalized as real. I often cannot convince someone that they are responding to shame, and to memory, even when they have been through it many times before.

Shame-based attacks on spouses may include physical violence, critical comments, threats of divorce, anger over mild transgressions, attempts to control, lying, and making circular arguments. These arguments begin with something so minor, neither can remember what it was by the time they are in my office. One person starts, the second reacts defensively (shame-induced), then the first reacts defensively. Each attacks in order to defend himself or herself. If neither felt shame the discussion would have begun and ended quickly. Circular arguments indicate that shame is interfering with relating.

Lisa's experiences in childhood are a good demonstration of how internalized shame early in life interferes with healthy marriages. She received intense shaming from the time she was born, and then layers were added on with rejection, sexual abuse, depression and consequent poor performance in school. When she began dating, she chose men like her abusive father, a common experience. She entered that bizarre situation in which she shamed the man, believing that he warranted it because he was abusive. If she had been able to set boundaries, she would have been healthy enough to not have entered into this relationship in the first place.

Pregnant with her first baby with Rob, she criticized him for not showing enough interest in the pregnancy; then after she gave birth, for his having no interest in preparing homemade baby food, and for finding her lacking in sex appeal.

Rob took on this shaming, as men do. But he grew to hate her for it, and expressed it in passive-aggressive ways. He would be late, or forget to buy something she needed, or insist on having the TV on very loud. He received shaming for this, too, and gradually became more overt in his retaliation. When he lost control and hit her, she decided that he was truly a bad person. Her family and his aligned with her against him. No one understood the role of her shaming in contributing to the creation of the nightmare. They divorced soon after.

When Lisa started therapy during her second marriage she was able to see that she picked sexually addicted men who could become violently angry. She began working on how she would choose a man who had qualities that didn't contribute to a loving relationship and then shame him for it. When she was able to clearly see her husband, and accept him for who he was, she stopped shaming him. Once she gave up the tight bond (called trauma bonding) that came from the back and forth abuse, she saw that he wasn't open to changing, and she was able to leave him.

Defensiveness Always Indicates Shame

Defensiveness is a shame-based reaction to feeling shame. If you weren't defensive, you would understand a shaming comment as a reflection of something going on with the other person.

If curious, you would want to know what he didn't like. You would evaluate his response and apologize, or explain how he misunderstood, or see that his objections aren't warranted and do nothing.

Curiosity is a shame-free feeling!

It's opening up and engaging in life. And it feels so much better than defensiveness. I practice noticing when I feel defensive, and instead try on curiosity. When I succeed, it's amazing! I can stop the shutting down that comes with shame-based anger.

If someone rudely says something like "What do you want?" he is in a bad mood, and you happen to be in front of him. Yet most people would join you in feeling angry and defensive about his rudeness.

Calling him rude allows you to feel less shame.

If you had no shame you could see that he is not a happy person and it isn't personal. We need to educate ourselves about small examples of defensiveness so we can become aware of our own shame.

As my informal shame study continued, I discovered that I could see my shame-laced patterns more and more clearly. When talking with a friend, I heard myself in an apologetic tone tell her that I thought I had told her this before. I don't need to apologize. I am going to tell her again anyway, so why mention the possibility that I had said it before? In the past I played out these patterns, and then apologized for having the pattern! What a waste of time and energy—and life! This is changing as my awareness has sharpened. I don't have to do anything more than just become aware. Change follows in its own time.

Examples of Defensive Shame

1) Her: You were an hour late, what's up?

Him in shame: Well, it wasn't my fault, the traffic was terrible and I had to stop for gas, I couldn't help it. You're always after me. I didn't do anything wrong.

Him out of shame: Yes, I am. I tried to call but my phone didn't go through. I'm sorry you had to wonder.

2) Him: I saw you flirting with another man. You hurt me.

Her in shame: What are you talking about, I wasn't flirting, I was just being friendly. I don't have any interest in him, what's wrong with you, you always think I'm after someone. You don't trust me.

Her out of shame: I was, wasn't I! I see how that hurt you. It isn't right to flirt when I'm in a relationship.

3) Him: You're not telling me the truth. You said you were at your friend's and I was told you were at a bar. Why did you lie?

Her in shame: What are you doing checking up on me? Don't you trust me? You never have believed me, why should I bother telling you the truth? You wouldn't believe the truth either. (Name calling is frequent here, along with defensiveness.)

Her out of shame: Yes. I lied. (pause) I think I was afraid you would judge me for having a drink with a friend and not inviting you. I shouldn't have lied. I'm glad you told me.

Shame and Anger Are Different

It seems necessary to differentiate shame from anger as most people feel shamed when someone is angry. Angry shaming isn't a valid expression of anger, and won't discharge it. It is a defense, used to avoid feeling one's own shame. Healthy anger meets a real need. Shaming doesn't. Healthy anger is straightforward, focused on the anger itself, with the intent of getting it out. Angry shaming uses a shaming tone, and is focused on the other person, not on the angry one. Regardless of the words, it communicates that the other person has done something seriously wrong.

Being Acceptable May or May Not Be Shame-Based

Our natural human motivation includes wanting to be acceptable to the community and to fit in. The healthy function of shame includes this because it supports the development of community. Toxic shame distorted this into having us believe that we will or will not be allowed to belong. In a shame-based culture we can only really fit in if we share the same rules for how to be.

When heavily in Avoidant Attachment, I couldn't fit in or feel as if I did. Now that I am healing shame and my need for separation, I find that there are wonderful ways to fit in that don't require following the rules of those I fit in with!

Healing shame makes it possible to live well and fit in
from a gentle, inwardly directed existence.

Feelings That Are Not Shame-Based

As human creatures, we come with the capacity to experience a range of emotions. All can be healthy expressions of our community-based nature. And all can become distorted from living in a shame-based culture.

Part of most people's day-to-day life is fear of feeling shame. Fear alerts them so they can maneuver to avoid it. However, some fear is not shame-based. Real fear, from narrowly avoiding a car accident, or seeing a child run into the street, is useful for staying alive and keeping the species going. During a recession, fear can assist in our taking steps to be safe. Fear from childhood or adult trauma is also not shame-based, even though from the perspective of the present, it is irrational. The well-known flashbacks of combat vets occur in people who have been abused in the past until they can heal those old hurts. Shame-distorted fear is considered normal but would not exist if we had no toxic shame. I believe this makes up most of the fear that humans experience. What a waste of time, and energy, and adrenal function, and life!

Shame can distort hurt, too. Hurt is a real feeling that occurs when one's monogamously bonded partner is sexual with others. Hurt alerts the betrayed one, and the expression of it can alert the betrayer that the activity is harmful. Like healthy shame and anger, it is a signal that integrity is off and something needs to change. But when the betrayed person adds shame to the hurt, it becomes difficult to heal. The hurt can go on and on even when its purpose has been served.

Anger is a powerful boundary-setter. When the other person doesn't respond to a calm statement of a limit, anger becomes necessary to get his or her attention. The extreme is seen in wars. In shame-free cultures, war would not be necessary as conflicts would be worked out. In our culture, anger occurs most often as a defense against shame. People who talk down to others, who control with the power of being a boss or with money, who shame others for not seeing things their way, trigger anger. If we had no shame we would shake our heads and walk away when others want to shame us into something. Psychotherapy clients love the times when they can finally stop reacting to a parent or spouse or boss.

Laughter is a wonderful emotion and very good for our physiology. But based on shaming, or being shamed, or making unhealthy jokes, it becomes a defense against shame.

Flirting is an energizing experience for single people who want to communicate an attraction to someone who is available. This is a healthy use of sexual energy. However, flirting is more commonly used to create an intensity that can't progress into possible romantic relating. This meaningless interest is employed to reduce the experience of shame because flirting implies that the object of it is attractive and valued. When the flirter goes on to flirt with someone else, the original object becomes angry or hurt, having lost the source of avoiding shame.

Even contentment or peace or satisfaction can be created in order to avoid the feeling of shame. For example, if you believe that someone is critical of you, or you are about to be sanctioned at work, finding out that you are wrong feels good. The shame disappears. Social drinking can permit a more enjoyable evening by reducing the experience of shame.

Recognizing Why Others Act the Way They Do

We are all confronted by strange behaviors of others, such as intense criticism, attack, withdrawal, denial of a problem obvious to everyone else, etc. If we can remember that irrational behaviors are the result of fear or shame, it makes it easier to understand what is going on.

We encounter other people's defenses against feeling their shame. Chapter 8 covers the numerous ways we inhibit the feeling of shame.

Chapter 8
Overriding the Experience of Shame

Every single one of us carries shame. Every single one of us uses a variety of methods to not feel it. *It is these avoidance maneuvers that prevent us from truly being ourselves and automatically knowing our integrity.*

These maneuvers are so entrenched in the culture, so integrated into cultural consciousness, that they are difficult to see. I have studied them for a very long time, knowing that I had to see them for what they are rather than believe they are normal facets of being human. What people mean by "the human condition" isn't human. It's the response to carrying shame.

Some of us have experienced such abuse and neglect in childhood that we carry too much emotional pain to avoid shame by using the culturally approved methods. We are forced to learn how to heal.

Most people can successfully override shame. They live their lives following the rules, proving they are good people, searching for the esteem of others, obtaining approval for who they are. Social drinking makes relating easier, gossip brings a sense of closeness. They can manage their shame by diminishing its intensity.

In the healing of shame, it is vital to observe how you avoid the experience. If you continue the avoidance, shame isn't available to be healed. I have provided a list of thirty-five common practices that are used to distract from shame, but please know that there are countless more. Each of us has found what works for our particular beliefs about ourselves, and so there are no universally applicable methods. I suggest that you look over the list to see which are common for you. Starting there, by observing how you use them, along with how you feel before you do and after, you can begin piecing together your network of avoidance mechanisms.

I found that some of my own practices were obvious, and I could decide to stop them. Yet other maneuvers became visible only when I had stopped using them! I didn't know they were shame avoiders until I no longer needed them to avoid shame!

And then there are the complicated ones that enhance life *and* avoid shame! For example, being married. Coupling and having children are obvious human instincts as they have occurred since recorded history in virtually all cultures. It is natural and reasonable for our species to perpetuate itself.

Marriage manages shame, too, as a convention to follow. Those choosing to be unmarried are not obeying the custom. Then there are those of us who elect Avoidant Attachment as a way to safely preserve ourselves, yet we still need closeness. Two Avoidant Attachers can marry, create what looks like a loving, typical family, yet live as emotionally separate as they did when growing up.

When I married at age twenty-two I was terrified to go out into the world on my own. I could not imagine a life centered on myself, on my professional interests and preferred living location. I needed someone. This can be seen as just fear—fear of being unable to make a life for myself, shyness that prevents creating a new social life, uncertainty in making good decisions.

My husband believed that his life was to include a wife and children and a dog. Only after we divorced did he realize that he much preferred a life with no wife or dog, and with a son, daughter-in-law and grandchildren to visit from afar.

My fear was of shame. The nature of this fear is like the fear of public speaking. It is irrational, even while strong and very real. My concern about going out in the world was the same. I could of course do it. I was intelligent, I knew how to apply for jobs I qualified for, I could live with my parents until I could support myself. There was nothing real to fear.

As an Avoidant Attacher, however, I lived as an alien. When in memory, I didn't know if I could understand what was needed, and then do it. An investment partner and I shared this irrational fear. We were both capable of making good investments, but by doing that together we were able to stay entirely unconcerned over our decisions. It was apparent that by having each other to reflect back to us the integrity of our decisions, we were able to plunge forward into a fascinating business. With shame out of the way we could both stay in the present. Then we could appreciate our unique skills. When problems came up, we breezed through them. I could see that my partner was in integrity with our decisions, and he could see that I was. As we were able to believe in each other, neither of us felt shame!

After so much healing, I can make these same investments without a shame-free mirror of myself. If I hadn't yet healed sufficiently, I would still work with someone else to quiet my shame. Why not, when I have available a guaranteed method of preventing shame from stopping me from doing something satisfying and lucrative? For the same reason, I plan exercise that requires setting up appointments. When arranging something with someone else, I am out in the world, in my real present-day life. If I were going out on a walk or bike ride alone, I might still not go. The old view of myself as an alien could re-emerge and prevent me from stepping forward in natural, self-caring ways.

When we have an inability to care for ourselves—to eat and exercise and carry out many activities that are not difficult—it is all shame-based! This is so common that it is hard to see that it isn't the nature of mankind. Instead, with shame gone, I get to have the amazing experience of gobbling down wonderful organic foods and feeling repulsed by any other kind! Now I know for sure that when I don't take good care of my body, it's shame!

Lisa worked hard to identify her shame and how she defended against it. It took a while for her to accept that shaming people was a ploy to avoid her own shame. Now she quietly explains what others are doing that is bad for her. She would have appreciated reading the book that a colleague is writing called, *If He Would Just . . .* which portrays how women want their men to change so they (the women) can feel good. Since this was her way to not feel reject-able, unlovable, and unloving, she would still have to find fault even with a perfect man. She only became free when healing that hideous shaming from rejection during gestation, and being wanted by no one until a stepfather valued her for sex.

While Lisa used many maneuvers to avoid shame, including being married, condemning men was the most disruptive. Along with many women, she obsessed over what her partner was doing that harmed her. When she criticized him for it, she didn't understand why he grew to hate her. This hatred became the next focus for condemnation.

She is now married to a man with some of the qualities of her first two husbands, but she understands that if she has boundaries around her time and activities, she won't have to criticize him. As her shame drops she is increasingly comfortable doing this. Boundaries are evidence of self-loving, like exercise and eating well. Shame interferes with the experience of loving oneself.

As you can see, our methods to avoid feeling shame are complex. They don't fit into a neat list like the one below. It is each person's job to observe his or her methods, allowing them to make sense over time. Many of mine are still not visible, and I have come to see that they may not be until they are no longer needed. I can heal shame without understanding all the ways I avoid it. However, if your defenses do a good job of preventing the experience of shame, you may be served by setting aside one or more in order to see what happens.

Ways We Use to Diminish Feeling Shame

As readers of this book in draft form repeatedly told me, I have not explained everything in sufficient detail for a beginner to under-stand. Truly explaining would take a whole book. Because of this, I invite you to gather together with your shame-healers and elaborate on each one yourself. While some may seem obvious from a paragraph or two, your own examples will further illuminate them.

For brevity's sake, I've listed only thirty-five ways people employ to diminish shame. There are truly hundreds, considering that each person develops his unique form of those below or discovers other forms. Since *observing* is the primary focus for healing, beginning with this list can be a powerful approach.

Criticizing

Putting others down is a powerful way to avoid shame. Finding someone else to be worthy of shame makes people feel as if they aren't. Thinking about how bad other people are helps them feel as if they are good. Stories on TV magazine shows and talk shows help viewers feel superior by portraying how awful something or someone else is.

Alcohol and Drugs

Even in small quantities, drugs and alcohol can alter bad feelings. An everyday example is the small group of people in a restaurant. Often they will be quiet until they have made it through most of their first drink, then they become happier and louder. Not alcoholics, they're ordinary shame-ridden people who enjoy turning it off for a while. Addiction is an extreme form of avoidance.

Taking Care of Others

Caretaking to feel like a good person, rather than for the innate pleasure of meeting real needs, or agreeing to a division of labor or conditions of employment reduces shame. When such actions become habitual, they are difficult to recognize for what they truly are, and difficult to confront. After all, how can you question caregiving?

Religion

Religion can be used to avoid feeling shame. Following rules that are clearly laid out by the highest authority offers security—if the rules can be followed. This backfires because it is hard, if not impossible, to comply with all the rules of "goodness."

The perception of Christianity as affirming that we are born bad and get to be redeemed can be a way of letting us off the hook. It wasn't our fault, we come that way. Then we get to work on how to make ourselves right and how to find integrity.

I believe that we were all born perfectly human and integrated into the big picture of everything. Then shame is laid on the child, beginning with attachment deprivation, followed by cultural shaming. Then emotions that heal are inhibited; for example, when a child is taught to not be angry and not cry. These essential emotions of grief are needed to heal trauma, shame included.

Because he can't entirely heal, the child becomes to some degree inhuman. This is why children fight, destroy property, compete, demand, bully, act like victims, and so on. Then they must override shame, or heal it, or suffer it. Sadly when religion is used to avoid shame, we can only employ rules for goodness instead of obtaining help with truly discovering our integrity.

Being Good

Most people try to do the right thing, to be considerate, suppress anger, etc., in order to consider themselves as good. Many value a reflection from others that they "have a heart of gold." They are "good people." They "would give you the shirt off their backs." This can defend against shame.

A sign on the window in Starbucks said, "Do something good every day." People like a rule or suggestion for how to feel good about oneself! Shame-free people don't need to think about doing something good—they just live, doing good things as a matter of course, without thinking about it. Shame-based people want to think that doing good things makes them good people—in other words, not shame-worthy.

Being Really Nice

While all of us have inherent desires to love and be helpful, appearing nice and good are classic ways that shame-based people use to obtain a positive, approving reflection from others. Niceness can be a good maneuver against shame. Those who use outside validation as an antidote want others to think they are nice because it means they aren't worthy of shame. Many clients have told me that their abusive fathers were well liked, as if this meant they couldn't really have been abusive.

Bradshaw says that being nice is hostile! It is a manipulation because it isn't really about either person. It uses others. The nice person cannot like having to be nice in order to relieve shame, and may take it out passive-aggressively on those he is nice to.

Following Rules

When trying to be good to avoid feelings of shame, a set of rules helps. Following the prescriptions of a church or family or community or sub-culture can make it is easier to establish that one is good. If they are vague it is more difficult. In this shame-based culture, it is difficult to live without rules, rather than operate out of integrity.

There are no rules for integrity.
Each of us has to heal it into existence.

Rationalizing

All people rationalize their behavior or thoughts in order to justify them as not shame-worthy. Typical rationalizations are: it wasn't my fault, he deserved it, he should have known better, he should have done something different, I didn't mean to do it. Or, it's your fault, if you hadn't done that I wouldn't have done what I did, if the laws weren't stupid I wouldn't have broken them.

I am imagining having a party where everyone sits around exaggerating rationalizations they have used or heard, and laughing hysterically! They really are funny if you don't need them or if they aren't directed at you.

Psychological Defense Mechanisms

In addition to rationalizing, other psychological defense mechanisms used to avoid shame and other painful experiences include: *repression* of feeling, *denial* of experience, *forgetting* something happened, *dissociation* from all feeling, thought or physical sensation, *reaction formation*, which may consist of feeling love to override hate, and many more. *Healing the Shame that Binds You* has a longer list with explanations of the use of defense mechanisms.

Becoming Congruent with Shame

Some people are so shame-laden that they can't escape. For them, it is effective to *become congruent with badness*. People who cheat, steal, and abuse others are living shamefully, which actually avoids shame. Alcoholics want to be with other heavy drinkers because they won't feel shame. They support each other's use of alcohol. If they drink with non-drinkers, the drinkers' shame will emerge.

Many of my clients, who are honest and trusted, had stolen and lied when they were teenagers. Some parents rationalize that their children got in with the bad crowd, but who are the bad crowd? Teens who feel great shame after years of torment find that "being bad" feels really good.

Sexual shame is a good example of a universal feeling that can be overridden by agreeing that sex is dirty or nasty. Some people are only capable of becoming aroused when they can see sex that way. Loving, or "good" sex, can be difficult. "Bad" sex includes pornography, prostitution, even illicit flirting. Loving, conscious sex brings up the shame that has become attached to sex. I have seen many couples where the man has no interest in sex with his wife once she stops being willing to act as if it were dirty. This has been called the Virgin/Whore dichotomy. Sex with the "good" woman brings up his shame, while sex with a "whore" doesn't, because it is shameful. He can be congruent with the shame.

Even when the woman continues to act as if sex were bad and dirty, men with a great deal of sexual shame often cannot be aroused. Healing sexual shame allows people to enjoy loving, healthy sex.

People who override shame with arousal find that orgasm will bring shame back. These are people who can't cuddle afterwards. They have to do something to avoid the discomfort of shame. I had a sexually addicted client who avoided orgasms. He masturbated so much that he would hurt his penis, but he would not have orgasms. He felt terrible when he was not aroused. We learned that he had been severely sexually abused by his father in childhood, which sexualized him and shamed sex.

Some people who abuse will later feel shame and remorse, seesawing back and forth between the two. Others can't tolerate the shame of remorse and are continually controlling of spouses and children and perhaps employees.

Men going out in groups to strip clubs or looking for one-night stands are supporting each other in being "bad." They are relieved of shame for a little while.

Seeing Others As Worse Than We Are

Attacking, judging others as worse than we are, and turning against a shamer by shaming all act to prevent feeling shame. Joining together to detail the badness of the others reinforces one's right to not feel bad about oneself.

When I walked into a coffee shop and noticed a woman looking me up and down critically, I knew that my clothing was being evaluated and it failed to measure up! I might have felt hurt or inadequate or as if I didn't fit in or just wrong, if my shame had been triggered. Her shame was medicated with the drug of condescension.

Hiding, Concealing, Lying

Deceit is an easy antidote to the fear of receiving shame. Just make something up so the other person thinks you are better than you think you are. Of course, when the lies are discovered far more shame arrives—from others and from internalized shame.

Lying develops as a defense against being found out by parents and punished. Since punishment also brings shame, it is to be averted. Once it becomes clear that lying can avoid shame, it becomes a habitual defense. Highly shamed people who needed to lie in childhood find that as adults they lie with no purpose. It has become habit, much as others smile habitually at everyone.

A friend long engaged in healing lied to me about where she was on the freeway when we were about to meet. Immediately after we got together, she told me. This kept us clear, showed me again that she values honesty, and helped her continue healing from the perceived need to lie.

False Self, Using Clichés

Mental health uses the term, false self, to describe people who have made up their experience so completely that they convey no sense of who they really are or what they are feeling. Some false selves use clichés to communicate so that the listener thinks he or she understands what is being said but actually isn't. If you listen closely, you can hear that clichés don't truly communicate. For example, if you tell a friend that you failed an exam. The friend says, *Everything is for the best.* What does this really communicate?

Everyone offers a desirable impression at times, of course. This is because we all carry shame.

A sex addict client offered a false self that prevented me from grasping his experience of life. He spoke warmly of loving his father, brothers, wife and children, yet I felt none of it. It was like watching bad acting.

When I described his false self he thought I was very strange. After four months I was about to tell him I couldn't see him any longer as no therapy was taking place. But then his wife caught him acting out his addiction and told him to move out. He fell apart, became real, and earnestly explored his addiction. Over months, he came to discern the components of his false self, and eventually became real most of the time. In fact, he became capable of empathy, of recognizing his intuitive knowing, and of loving in a communing manner. And of course he was much happier.

Being Apologetic when It Is Unnecessary

Apologizing is appropriate when we have done something hurtful. It is our way of acknowledging that we were out of integrity and now see that it was harmful. Healthy shame motivates the apology, and once it is complete, we return to normal.

However, most apologizing isn't based on truly doing something that warrants it. The young woman sitting in the big Starbucks chair next to mine moved her things way over to her side of the table between us when I sat down. She said to tell her if she was in my way. This was unneeded because I had far more room than necessary. She put me in a position of forgiving her before she did anything I wouldn't like. This is an effective defense.

Apologizers prevent others from shaming them,
and so they
prevent themselves from feeling internalized shame.

A man I know communicates by tone, facial expression, and body language that he is always on the verge of feeling shame. He will later apologize for something he said that wasn't offensive. He does that when he needs a de-shame hit. It has nothing to do with the other person. He doesn't even need to be forgiven; just the act of apologizing is his drug. It does the job.

Notice how you respond when others over-apologize. Do you lean forward and earnestly tell them it's okay?

Manipulating and Controlling

Working on others to get them to do what you want can come from a number of motives. One is to avoid shame. The person who decides how things are, and manipulates the family or business to do it her way, can believe that she is never wrong or stupid.

Contrast the feeling of being in control and getting others to do what you want with the feeling of being shameful, bad, inadequate, and not worthy of life. If you had to face the latter on a regular basis, wouldn't you prefer the former? It feels so much better to think one is knowledgeable and right and powerful.

People who use manipulation as an avoidance maneuver actually bring on more shame, because others don't like to be controlled. Many women go to therapy to learn how to set boundaries and not be controlled. This is threatening to the controller. If we as a community can understand that people are merely trying to make life manageable, we don't have to shame them for it. Instead, we can just not let them control.

Triangulating against "Bad" People

Making others bad in order to feel like a better person is a common method of avoiding shame. The larger the number of people gathering together against a person or a group, the more effective is the shame medication. Racism involves many people focusing hatred toward many others. Nationalism is, too, even when other nations are considered allies. Feeling separate, and better, is useful in avoiding shame. Being part of a media community in hating a murderer or pedophile avoids feeling shame. *That person is so bad—so much worse than I am.*

Politicians, economic leaders, athletes, and celebrities who are doing something that engenders disapproval are put down in a helpless, shaming fashion. Documentaries and news articles exploit this kind of story because it sells.

Gossip

Gossip is the individual, or small-group, form of triangulation. People gossiping together use the emotions of shock, criticism, and shaming to bond with each other. This is a form of trauma bonding, where trauma emotions are used to create bonds when healthier forms aren't available.

Gossip is such an integrated facet of American life that even when people intellectually understand that they will also become the object, they wouldn't consider stopping. When they are the object, they will feel angry and violated. The roles of gossiper and gossipee are compartmentalized in order to reduce the experience of shame, and isolation, and being left out, and not fitting in.

Staying Busy

Being busy is a major, effective tactic to avoid shame, popular in our high-speed world. With too much to do and not enough time, there is no room to check inside and see what is going on in there. Addiction treatment programs look at a person's lifestyle. If you can't check in with yourself, there is no way to be alerted when addiction rears up, and then to interrupt it. One can be busy with work, family, anything that enables over-commitment.

Cell phones, texting, the use of the Internet for electronic games, chat rooms, porn sites and more are all common tools for those who wish to stay away from shame.

Romanticizing

Romanticizing might be described as a bright-eyed, sighing exclamation over something perceived as really really important. A client said she just knew that in the new year she would become healthy, she would do those prescribed tasks that would finally bring health. She didn't. The commitment wasn't real. She was only using the anticipation to interrupt shame.

A woman prayed to get a sponsee in her 12-step program, and when a woman in the afternoon meeting asked her to be her sponsor, the first woman jumped up and down, exclaiming that the second woman made her day. She made up that the prayer and the event mean far more than they do. Instead of seeing that she communicated a readiness for a new experience, and then found that experience, she took it to verify her ability to control god, to decide what she wanted and obtain it.

Television commercials romanticize. They overdraw the value of what they promote. They attempt to get you to pay more attention, feel good, and thus purchase. Ad creators study people to see what gets attention and cooperation. Advertising might as well say: Buy or use this in order to reduce your shame. In truth, the vast majority of sales would not take place if we had a shame-free culture.

In a movie, a woman told her husband, You will be a wonderful father, and having a baby will be the best thing that could happen to us. Her tone conveyed emphasis and drama. She was creating false, romanticized emotions in the present to predict the future.

When romanticizing getting a new job, or into a good college, it's disappointing to discover that it is just life, just one day after another, and hard work. When we think that the event is the answer, we set ourselves up for disappointment. This won't occur if we see accurately. This would mean feeling glad for the job or the college acceptance, but knowing that it is only a door into what is possible. Life is only this very day, this moment.

*Romanticizing creates a
roller coaster of made-up emotion.*

Broadcasting Sexual Energy

Sexual energy is ours to use when bonding with a partner, for continuing the exclusive bond, and for feeling good in private. Any other transmission, as with wearing revealing clothing, is to obtain reactions from others in order to feel powerful, controlling, attractive, valuable, present, successful, and a host of other antidotes to shame. If someone who is not available flirts with you, she really has no personal interest in you. She is trying to use you to feel something about herself.

Stylized Friendliness

Some people create a very friendly, interested persona. If you are on the receiving end you might wonder why you don't enjoy such friendly people when they seem so very interested in you. It may be because they are really not interested. They are merely trying to avoid shame.

Some friendly people are very good actors and able to convince you that you truly are interesting. This feels different from the real, less intense, communing interaction that is truly human—and truly friendly.

Dressing in Style or by the Rules

This is an excellent example of how people spend money and a great deal of time working hard to prove they have no reason to feel shame. Because it is so prevalent, I didn't think much about it until my clients started coming to sessions in Southern California heat wearing calf-high boots lined with fur—the very same boots we wore years ago in Alaska for warmth that were seen as unattractive but necessary.

Is there anyone who truly dresses to feel comfortable? Some might think that people who wear old, torn clothes might be free of social shaming. But they are either rebelling against the rules, or they live in so much shame that it really doesn't matter to them what they wear. They aren't able to push shame aside with clothing. Taking care of one's body, including putting on clean, neat clothes, is natural when living shame-free. Choosing lovely colors and textures can come from non-shame living.

The phrase, "looking presentable," implies shame if one is not dressed and acting according to societal rules.

Being "Beautiful"

Billions of dollars are spent on plastic surgery for cosmetic purposes. Research found that breasts now considered most sexy are those created with implants. Clothing, working out, hair, makeup, skin treatments, Botox, and surgery are used by people who think they will be more valuable, and thus have less shame, when they look as good as possible. People rarely think they have succeeded, because the shame that caused it is still there. With no shame, they wouldn't think that these services added to their value.

Trite Explanations of Life

When people say: it was meant to be, there's a reason for every-thing, or, it's god's will, they are tidying up their experience in artificial ways. Such explanations take away personal responsibility, and thus personal shame. While these "truths" may be true, speaking them has the function of relieving the other person's shame. People can by-pass fear of the consequences of their choices and decisions because these sayings explain anything away. However, they interfere with the grief that is necessary to release past pain in order to live in the present.

The expressions, "making a difference" and "giving something back," are romanticized, shame-medicating statements. They are out-side-in definitions of goodness. If we were shame-free, we would auto-matically help meet others' real needs, and never even think about it. It would feel good because we are community creatures who receive pleasure from living congruently with our nature.

Giving back is based on some kind of record-keeping. I was given to, and so I give to others. My own experience of giving is that it feels really good to give when meeting real needs. I love that I have devel-oped skills to give well in my profession. But why think of it as giving back? This is a distorted view of gratitude, a rule that receiving help must be followed by an appreciative helping back. In a shame-free cul-ture we would all be helping all the time, and we would all be receiving help all the time. It is sad that people can be so cut-off from that know-ing that they resort to a romanticized desire to somehow feel good about themselves.

This is simple: If I enjoy helping, I will help. Period. *The goal of helping others serves the need to override shame.* It becomes part of one's identity of goodness.

Magical Thinking

Creating false beliefs and practices in order to ameliorate the ex-perience of shame leads people to believe things are true that are not. Then other, non-shame related events are taken as true because of the diminished ability to differentiate.

When a credit card company lost a class action suit, it sent checks to everyone who had been defrauded by the company. A client, who had borrowed a great deal of money on credit cards, received a sizable check. She told her therapy group that this was evidence she was doing good things, perhaps good work in therapy. She believed that there was a direct connection between getting this money and what she had done. This is a great distortion of the concept of karma, often used as a throw-away reason for many things going wrong. Or right.

Looking for information about what is going to happen or what one should do is a typical source of distortion. A client who believed that bluebirds are a sign of rightness looked out my window to observe a blue jay, and she assumed with a smile that the decision she had been pondering was the right one. When people look for signs, or see signs, they aren't trusting that they already have the information. They may not be able to look within and check out their intuition, their knowing. Shame prevents it.

Develop (or Copy) Values to Live By

When we uncover our natural understanding of being social creatures, knowing how to relate to others is automatic. Healthy shame alerts us if we stray. I want to not lie, to respond to real needs of others, work hard for things of value to me and others, find my role in the community, develop my abilities and interests and see how they serve, expand myself in whatever ways show up as right for me, learn what integrity is and enjoy operating within it, and much more.

This list might be seen as values to live by, but it isn't. I just live it, automatically, without thought. I don't do these things because they are good, or because they make me a good person. I do them because that's who I am. My toxic shame hasn't prevented me from staying with myself.

When my mother was in a nursing home, and I held power of attorney, I was confronted with discovering the difference between accepting responsibility for a parent and giving guilt-ridden attention. By remaining open to this question, I found that I was fully motivated to take care of her finances and make other decisions. Every moment doing this was spent feeling good and alive with no resentment. However, I didn't visit her to be a good daughter or a good person. My siblings did. I was able to override the voices speaking in my head about what is right, so when she died I had absolutely no regret. It wasn't right for me to act loving with a parent who had not loved me and who had not received my love. Perhaps it was right for my siblings.

Religion offers rules to follow in order for us to live up to the values of the culture. Bradshaw uses the term, religiosity, to mean the use of religion to handle shame by following rules and criticizing others for not following them. This is in contrast to using religion to evolve into a less shame-based life.

The term, *belief system*, has the same quality as values in that it is *made up because of having lost the intuitive understanding of how to live*. We have to have beliefs when we don't have access to a natural understanding. Values and belief systems will fall away when they are no longer needed.

You can imagine how awkward it is when someone tells me that they are doing something because of their values, or tells me that I have strong values! I will usually say it isn't a value, or I don't have values.

Humor Used to Avoid Shame

Humor relieves shame. I watched an Eddie Murphy video with the audience in hysterics. All he did was say sexual words and walk around the stage, giving permission to people to laugh. I didn't find it funny as I had specialized in sexuality for a long time, and had healed most of my sexual shame, so I didn't need humor to hear the words and know what they meant. Sex, elimination, farting, failure, saying the wrong thing, not knowing the answer and so on can be de-shamed with humor.

Writers who say that it is good to be able to laugh at ourselves are referring to self-shaming. We wouldn't laugh at ourselves or others if we didn't need to lighten the feeling of shame. Laughing at ourselves might help while we are learning the causes of our shame and becoming able to see them more clearly. Eventually, freedom from shame would include freedom from laughing at anyone.

When shame isn't limiting us, humor emerges in the simplest activities, expressing the joy of life. *The Continuum Concept* describes men laughing their way through difficult, even painful, physical tasks. Laughter adds energy in the same way that controlled out-breathing and moaning allow increased access to physical strength. This humor acknowledges that this is a right thing to do even if it is hard.

When playing racquetball with my favorite partner, we laugh our way through the games! When we get a long rally going, getting shots we thought weren't possible, we laugh! We are delighted no matter who gets it. When one of us makes a bad shot, we don't laugh at ourselves, we just move on to the next serve.

Greed

Doesn't it make sense that greed would seem like an antidote to being deprived of real love and attention and success and integrity and community and belonging? It can be a search to obtain what one never had, and may appear to be a solution to the shame brought about by the deprivation.

Greed seeks to prove that
one is worth having what is sought.

Secondarily, it tries to prove that one is superior, smarter, better and successful. We see examples of greed that have created great wealth and control over others. Gambling addicts fail to achieve the benefits of greed. They alternate between the ecstasy of seeming to win mommy's attachment and the devastation of losing it. Instead of healing shame, gambling heaps it on.

Falling in Love

If we don't naturally have love all around us, then falling in love holds great appeal. The cultural draw is intense, reflected in movies, TV and novels. The series, "Sex in the City," dramatically portrayed how four women who cared for each other and supported each other through anything could so easily couple with men just because that's what one should do. They "fell in love," but there was always something wrong with the man, and he was soon dispensed with—until the end of the series, when magically, each woman found the right one.

Falling in love relieves the experience of shame for a time because both people are smitten. If someone is madly in love with you, you must be lovable after all! Then, when feelings subside, and the relationship falls into the ordinary, one or both can feel unloved. When falling-in-love is over, shame returns. Couples come to my office angry and critical of each other for no longer loving the way they did in the beginning. It's my job to help them see what they were after, and how healing themselves is more productive than trying to get the partner to become what they want.

Most falling-in-love is not based on real caring, on the expansion of life, of truly adding to life. No one with toxic shame is capable of engaging in such a pure manner. I want to jump up and shout to everyone, It won't work! Don't think it will work! Please, stay with yourself, learn how to heal shame, see how you medicate it, know that real love doesn't medicate it. *Real love makes you feel shame* because real emotions invite the healing of false ones.

Impersonal Sex

One outcome of internalizing shame, and defending against it is difficulty having love and intimacy. If we are making ourselves up, hiding who we think we are, while yearning to be cared for, we will have difficulty communicating accurately who we are and what we experience. We will also have difficulty receiving real communication from others. When two people are together trying to talk, they will sense how present the other person is. As the distance increases, they will try to create methods to feel close. Sex is commonly used for that—including with strangers.

Even less personal than sex with strangers is sex with pornographic images and fantasy. We know that much discomfort when having sex can be from sexual abuse in childhood, and then adult sex replays the horrible emotions occurring back then. Impersonal, addictive, trance-based sexual acts can avoid those old emotions. And they can avoid the shame that was created by those betraying abuses.

Being in a Relationship

Single people are not living the right life, according to the culture's rules, and are consequently expected to feel shame. This forces many people to fall in love, or at least get married. The rule has to be broken before it's possible to live alone and discover what surfaces needing to be healed. It is possible to not need a relationship so that having one is *only an addition to a good life.*

Having Children

I believe that coupling and having children is the right way to live, according to our genetic, community-creature instincts. It makes sense that two people bond tightly with sexual energy in time for the arrival of the babies that sex brings. Two people dividing the labor increase chances of the infant's survival. Of the many birds that bond for life, the ones I've observed work together to feed the babies. The albatross on Kauai are a lovely example of how the parents trade off sitting on the egg and tending the chick while the other parent goes diving for food.

In Southern California, quail chicks number over fifteen when tiny and silent, with about half remaining when reaching adult size. The full-grown chicks need caretaking for a period, and they walk along with the parents who speak quietly to them.

Shame-based people have babies for less optimal reasons. Some women want someone who will always love them, or for something to do, or to get or keep a man, or to have an object on which to project their hatred and shame so they can stop feeling them for a time. When babies pick this up they carry the shame of being used, unloved, and overtly shamed. Then they believe it is about them, not the parent.

Rote Living

Avoiding internalized shame brings many people to live by rules and habits and by imitating others.

Many habitual behaviors are valuable for leading an orderly life, such as showering and brushing teeth, eating breakfast, and countless others that don't require thought. At the same time, all of us develop habits that actually interfere with spontaneous choice.

I admired my mother-in-law's sweater, and she said she liked it, too. She added that she wished she had a better figure under the sweater, more up here and less down there, but you can't have it all. She wasn't really feeling badly about this, she was following a long prac- ticed habit. Later she looked at my computer, and when I said I was having trouble getting my e-mail, she said, Oh, you will! Both of these responses are not based on what is going on, they are stereotypical reactions to a situation or an emotion.

Many spouses depend on spending evenings with each other and have difficulty when one starts spending time away from home. Sensi- bly, the at-home spouse should have a life of his own so that he carries on with it even when his partner is gone. Single people figure this out with no problem.

Discussion in shame-healing groups can center on each person's exploration of habits that serve life and those that make life feel mean- ingful in an unreal way.

Becoming Disciplined

Discipline is necessary in order to work against obstacles that shame creates. If we had access to our full experience of life, we wouldn't need discipline. I have been told I have it, but I don't operate from any kind of motivator that feels like discipline. I follow my Feet. They take me in directions that lead me closer to being shame-free and able to love as fully as possible. As my shame drops, my ability to love grows. Then I automatically operate differently. I don't *try* to love. I don't *decide* to love. I don't set goals. I don't have values to live up to.

Somehow I knew that I needed to heal from my mother's view of me as entirely evil. But knowing was obviously not enough. I have followed my Feet for many years, one step, one task after another to educate myself about who we are as humans. Twenty years ago a friend asked me what would be the name of the book if I wrote what I was thinking, and I immediately said, *The Natural Order of Things*. While I haven't written a book by that title, it is the focus of my learning. At last, my understanding of the role of shame in each individual's life and in the culture has shown me so much more of the natural order of things. It has shown me what humanness really is. It has also shown me how to get there! And helped me to see why the journey is so very hard.

Healing Shame

As you set out on this task, naming those ways you use to avoid experiencing this emotion will help you discover what it is you are avoiding. People have earnestly told me that they don't feel shame even while I see obvious evidence that they not only feel it, but have created complex maneuvers to avoid knowing that they feel it. If this is true for you, then the first task might be seeing how you defend against shame, and stopping one or two methods for a short while to see what happens.

Chapter 9
Love and Community as They're Meant to Be

The previous chapters addressed the myriad facets of shame and their effects on individuals. Now we can take a look at what community might be like if toxic shaming were *not* integrated into everyday life. *The Continuum Concept*, by Leidloff, offers excellent information about what a shame-free culture is like. The author describes the healthy culture of a tribe that she lived with in South America. It offers a model of how we are intuitively guided to interact and the life that would be possible as a result.

Dorothy Bryant offered her views in a novel, *The Kin of Ata Are Waiting for You*. Bryant introduces a culture that beautifully integrates unique gifts and qualities into a fluidly working community. This shame-free functioning offers healing to a man who has all the worst characteristics of shame-driven people. He rapes, uses, discards, and eventually murders. He struggles against the members of this community but finally comes to understand. He heals his shame and develops his unique gift.

Our Unique Selves Integrated into Community

When we are fully ourselves, fully boundaried and fully able to release all boundaries appropriately, then we can join in community with others with no sacrifice, no controlling, no being controlled. Love and our innate positive understanding of how to work well together have a chance to emerge. The self is valued and supported, and communes with the self of everyone else.

Each unique person, separate from everyone else,
can totally merge into community

with no loss of the self.

Leidloff describes how babies in the South American tribe were held as long as they wanted while mothers went about their daily tasks. People laughed together as they completed difficult projects. No one acted like victims or abusers or rescuers. They didn't need to, because they had not lost their ability to commune. One man returned after a long time in the city and enjoyed sitting around, taking advantage of everyone else's labor. He had lost touch with the natural understanding of his people. They talked about him with concern, hoping he would come to see that having a good life meant joining the community, doing his part, giving what was good for him to give. They were *pleased for him* when he came to this understanding and began farming.

Each of us can heal shame in order to access natural instincts that members of this tribe followed. Solutions to all of our community and world problems would then naturally unfold.

Communing

I have come to recognize the feeling of being joined in the present with another person—communing. I have a sense of being in my whole body, my whole being. Nothing is cut off, pushed to another direction, squeezed aside. I breathe fully. I feel everything. The person or people I am communing with feel the same. We can do this when shame isn't operating. When it reappears, we return to typical, more separated interaction.

Secure Attachment

A healthy, shame-free culture would provide secure attachments for all children. The child's needs would be met first by the primary caregiver, usually the mother. As he becomes social and then mobile, his attachment would expand to include the father and other adults.

Research indicates that the secure bond is a natural product of being human and provides the best backdrop for adult life.

People without shame can fully perceive this need. If all parents were shame-free, and thus had access to intuitive understanding of the needs of humans at all ages, all children would be provided with a secure attachment! Leidloff's observations support this.

I have described attachment styles in past chapters. The style of attachment formed by the child with its primary caregivers influences how he will relate with attachment figures in adult life—and how he might handle acculturated shaming. When children are offered the opportunity for secure attachment, they interpret that as meaning something about them. Born with instincts that tell them what to expect from life, they will comfortably merge into the family, safely knowing their needs are met, and quickly exchange lots of love. Babies enter the community immediately!

Supported by a secure bond, the child has the freedom to travel along at the prescribed developmental pace, reaching each natural milestone in time: rolling over, standing, tearing paper, walking, talking, running away from Mom and then quickly back to her, counting, socializing, and all the way through school into adult developmental tasks. As she goes through the timely exploration, her unique gifts and interests and abilities appear. She gets to place importance on her personal explorations and develop them along with the shared tasks. The needs of the community will also flavor the development of her offerings.

If a person has received sufficient attention to his needs as an infant and in childhood, with parents who were able to perceive his communications, he will grow up feeling securely attached to them and others. This doesn't ensure emotional health, but it provides a valuable foundation.

The securely attached person is capable of
being well integrated into the family
and into the culture.

Outgrowing the Need for Attachment

A normal course of attachment obeys the real needs of the child. At birth he is entirely dependent, having to trust that his mother will be there for his every need. This includes love and relating as he is welcomed into life in community. He will instinctively use angry crying to get her attention if she strays, bringing her awareness back to him. When he learns to walk and can feed himself, then his attachment need is for safety, and for availability when he seeks love and reassurance.

By the time he is five he requires very little having bonded with adults and peers. At nine he needs a home and meals and boundaries, as his attachment with friends grows. He has entered community. By adulthood, he has outgrown his need for attachment to his parents, providing his own meals and shelter, and now depends on all around him for love and communing. When ready, he couples with another person and creates his own family. His relationship with parents and siblings changes. Parents become grandparents to his children, and eventually he has the responsibility to care for them. Affection and shared history remain, along with membership in the larger community.

In our culture of social isolation, family has taken on too much significance. It is difficult to outgrow that attachment because we cannot replace it with a solid community. Having a spouse and children is the closest we can come.

We also find it difficult to outgrow the need for attachment because none of us had one that is perfectly secure. Society prescribes putting the baby in his own bed as an infant and carrying him in a carrier. He is raised by parents with so much shame they can't sufficiently access themselves in order to entirely access the child's needs. They are not capable. This means that no one can have a truly secure attachment.

The more secure the attachment, the more easily the child can outgrow it, move into leading his own life, and create a larger community of friends, family and colleagues. Difficulty in outgrowing the need leads even healthier children to take on the values of the family, the school and the church in ways that don't serve them. A truly securely attached child would be able to grow into his innate understanding of humanity, develop his gifts in correct ways and attach to the community as a whole.

The adult who has grown out of childhood attachment will know what to do when his parents age and approach death. He will become responsible when it is appropriate. He will perceive their real needs and meet them. He won't do this because of the rules, or to feel like a good person or even because he loves them. He will access innate knowing that this is what humans are to do. It is part of our inherent integrity.

Vital Connection

Love is a central quality of human life that brings us true awareness of being alive and in community with others. Love brings pleasurable responsibility for meeting the real needs of others and satisfaction when we do. The pleasure of parenthood comes from taking on the needs of the baby as our own. It is so strong that, when we have little shame, it offsets the immense difficulty of caring for a being that demands everything all the time. *Pleasure when meeting real needs is who we are as humans.* We will do so unless shame or other obstacles prevent our satisfaction.

Healing individual and cultural shame
allows us to become human.

We have all had experiences in which the pressure of shame was lifted, and we became able to access our humanness for a while. Natural disasters connect people, providing a deep sense of togetherness and love—communion. Earthquakes, fires, floods, and hurricanes bring us together. 9/11 in particular united and connected us. We briefly got to experience the community that is our human heritage.

Singing or chanting together in large numbers, attending concerts, and even movies in theaters allow us to join with others for a while. They take us out of ourselves more completely than when we watch on TV because so many join in the experience.

The tragedy is that we don't get to commune all the time when involved with the simple tasks of life—food, shelter, transportation, exchange of goods and services, and all the basic needs.

The night Barack Obama was elected to the presidency millions of us cried together, touched by this amazing event. The *magnitude* of it *brought all of us together* even while we were spread out around the world. The strength of the shared feeling *stopped our shame*! With shame out of the way, we became human!

But it couldn't last. Shame and blaming others and divisiveness will prevail because individuals need that to stop the experience of shame. I cried through the inauguration for the coming together but also with grief because this was rare and temporary.

Wars can create unity. The population bands together to fight a justified cause. When a war becomes unpopular, those for and those opposed bond against each other.

Working well together is the natural state of humans. We are designed to love, and accept love, and help each other, and create *a well working order that supports the best in everyone.* So why is this rare? Why do we depend on emergencies, weddings, illness, injury, natural disasters, and death of loved ones in order to feel communally engaged? Why can't we have this experience all the time? Why do we have to use intensity to override the obstacles?

The answer is: *Internalized toxic shame permeates the culture.*

Healthy Shame and Guilt

The healthy forms of shame and guilt are mild emotions that flow through us, alerting us to what we need to do to support love and cooperation and pleasure and meeting the real needs of others in the community.

John Bradshaw writes about healthy shame, seeing it as a complex motivator to do well and live according to one's values. I see it as simply a soft, gentle pull forward toward serving ourselves, and in so doing, serving our community, our country, our world. The absence of war would be natural. Of course we wouldn't kill each other or rob each other's resources.

I went into a very crowded store to pick up my computer. I thought all I had to do was walk in and have it handed to me as I had already paid for it. The man who said he would help me helped two other people first. I interrupted him to say that all I wanted was to pick up my computer. He went to get it. The process took ten minutes while he got the computer out, turned it on, and had me check my data transfer. Now I saw that of course I shouldn't have been helped before others who were there before me. I told him I wanted to apologize for my attitude as I hadn't known it would take that time. I had no toxic shame. I could see that he was owed an apology or an explanation. I could right my implied criticism, which was out of order.

Regardless of how he responded, I felt good. I had returned to my well lubricated cells all working together. Period. The interesting thing is that I was pulled to do this, not pushed by shame. I felt better, cleaner, and in my integrity. I removed an obstacle to the pleasure of my day. I did it for me! And because I wasn't operating from toxic shame, making amends or asking to be forgiven, I could give him a gift of the two of us being together, working on this task. When I am in my integrity, I can care and give.

When shame is healthy, it is not unpleasant.

Parenting can come from this free, open place, too. Words like sacrifice and meeting the child's needs instead of your own are the result of being cut off from our humanness by shame. When parents have none, and know their integrity, they take on the child's needs as meeting their own. I *needed* to take care of my son. I didn't do it to be good, to follow rules, to do what's right. There was no sacrifice, no compromise. I did it because I needed to. This was true even though parenting was frightening, exhausting and demanding.

Being Alone or *Feeling* Alone

When people are fully engaged in community, no one will feel alone or lonely when by themselves.

Feeling alone or lonely is a symptom of unhealed shame. It is also a symptom of living in a culture dominated by toxic shame, which prevents communing, and leaves every one of us alone even with "loved ones."

"Alone" really means being away from who we are,
taking on the definitions of others,
believing the made-up world of those around us.

Authentic Need of Others

Living in community includes needing each other. Division of labor, having babies and bringing home food for the family have been experienced in community over the centuries.

We have a need to be seen and the need to see others—intimacy. This is a vital ingredient of being human, and necessary in order to create community that serves all. This is the kind of relating that we were designed to have. We require an honest reflection of ourselves and all of life in the eyes of others. We need to join in the task of creating and improving community. When we don't have this, we are alone.

If true humanness means being needed for who we are,
for being entirely ourselves,
then we are all deprived.

What does that do to us?

Non-Humans' Full-Life Experience of Community

When living in Hawaii, I made friends with wild chickens. I watched them, saw how they addressed fear, and how they got over it. Gradually I interacted with them until I was able to lie on the ground and scoot toward a hen warming her brood under her wings. She let me touch the chicks without pecking me—unheard of.

I tamed chicks so that I could hold them on my hand while they ate. When I was relaxed and comfortable, they were glad to do this. But if I was even slightly tense, they would fly down. What an example of the ability of animals to know what is going on with others! Did they learn this from their feet on my hand, or was it a larger energy they perceived? We are also prey. Don't we have this ability too? How was it squashed out of us? How can we reclaim it?

I also tamed many wild cats. They don't hide their fear or their desire for love or their immense pleasure when able to feel safe on a lap. Each one came closer for a few days, then disappeared for a week or so, then returned for increasingly more intimate relating. Each cat repeated this for more than a year until appearing more like house-raised domestic cats.

Brilliant yellow, black and green gold finches come to a feeder right outside my living room window. Colors flash as they take turns, turning their heads in all directions while swallowing the seed they have picked out of the sock. Of course they are vigilant! Prey have to pay attention to predators. This is a basic natural truth of their existence. They haven't been shamed into ignoring it! Their boundary is flight.

Myna birds in Hawaii gather at dusk and talk on and on as they move around in trees, swapping branches, until falling asleep at dark. They talk again on awakening. The huge banyan tree in Lahaina on Maui attracts thousands.

The albatross on the north shore of Kauai evolved with no predators, and so did not develop an instinctive fear of large animals. They express only mild concern when people walk right up to them.

None of these creatures lost their instinctive knowing of how to live. We can heal our way back to that.

Chapter 10
Shame Is the Root of World Problems

Now that I have delineated the subject of shame, I am adding these next pages that were initially the introduction. This overview of the magnitude of the harm caused by shame brought me to write the book, and I remain fascinated with increasing my understanding of the pervasive nature of this emotion.

Thinkers of all kinds have long tried to understand why our world is filled with violence, with blindness to the plight of others and the ultimate abuse of humanness—war.

The reason is very simple. Shame. Not the gentle emotion that rights us, that brings us back into symmetry with those around us. It's toxic shame, that intense unpleasantness that dominates every one of us and is passed along from generation to generation.

Toxic shame is that dreadful feeling of badness, of harming, of being unacceptable, of not belonging, of not being good enough. It's stomach-clenching, skin-crawling sensations. It is something we all know, we all feel. It will quiet down, and then leap up when we are criticized or feel that we have done something wrong or stupid or harmful or against the rules. It can appear from just being alive.

People don't know they are dominated by shame because our culture is full of methods to avoid feeling it. As I itemized in Chapter 8, the methods include shaming others, raging, niceness, flirting, being successful, winning, staying busy, being good, addictions, gossiping, and all defensive maneuvers.

As they prevent our feeling shame, they inhibit all other emotions and experiences, too. This limits our humanness, inhibiting our ability to live in peace, to easily solve conflicts, love children, develop our gifts and offer them to the community, and follow our instincts and intuition. As long as toxic shame is passed along in the culture over time, we as a people cannot fully find ourselves. We must know ourselves in order to identify our integrity and live appropriately.

In the struggle to avoid feeling deep, internalized shame by cutting ourselves off from other emotions, too, *we are left with an abbreviated version of humanity even while yearning for the full experience.* Then we create a version of emotions that resembles the ones we have abandoned. This is why movies offer made-up romance and love and family and caring and grief and happiness and protection and salvation and redemption. We get to step into strong emotions that we have inhibited in ourselves.

When we cut ourselves off from intuitive knowing of
love and support and respect and community,
then we can no longer see that
killing in the name of righteous war
is incompatible with our human instincts.

Instead, we can justify anger and hitting others, including children. Rape and child molestation become easier because healthy shame and guilt go underground, becoming inaccessible. Conscience is diminished. We live by habit instead of internally motivated integrity. Then we shame children without knowing we are harming.

When we live outside of integrity, even more shame is added on. Then we must suffer even more distancing from our true knowing and humanness.

The avoidance of the experience of shame underpins much damaging behavior in our community: bad parenting, poor work cultures, argumentative marriages, crimes, and war. It is the cause of bad economies, of poverty, of passive-aggressive actions, of holding each other accountable for our difficulties, and practically anything in the news. It causes depression and anxiety and fear. It leads people to believe that solutions must include lying, stealing and taking advantage of each other.

Here's the wonderful thing: Shame can be healed! When it is, the world will be righted.

This means that war and domestic violence and harming children can be stopped!

If every person set out to heal shame by no longer shaming, no longer receiving shame, and by discharging the internalized forms, the world's population would get on track and live according to our shared instincts.

We are born full of love and life, with the programming to discover our talents and gifts and develop them in ways that support community. We are capable of empathy, of seeing and being seen, of healing ourselves and others, of knowing how to be together without conflict. Shame is the pain that prevents us from accessing all of this. As I and my friends and clients heal our internalized toxic shame, we are discovering that it is possible to walk easily in the world, openly smiling and seeing and respecting others. Without internalized shame, we don't react to being shamed! Setting boundaries is effortless.

Self-help books, religion, and spiritual practices are geared to help people discover themselves and live happier lives. Each offers some improvement. However, since shame is the underpinning of difficulties, addressing the existence of it within the culture—and within each of us—is needed for comprehensive healing of each individual.

Chapter 11
How Does Shame Cause War?

World Peace

How *does* shame cause war?

All of us are medicating shame, and it feels best when we join with others to do so. We start with another person—a spouse or child or boss—and shame them to avoid our internalized shame. This helps, but it is more effective if done with others. Gossip was invented for this function—the two of us against them.

Even more effective is when one country goes against other countries, judging and criticizing them for being different and strange and wrong. This evolves into nationalism, and racism, where those who appear one way condemn those who appear another. This makes us believe that we belong, that we are connected to a large number of people. The larger the number, the more right we feel, as our views are reflected back to us by so many. The larger the condemned group, the greater the effectiveness in warding off shame. When one whole group shames another whole group, it is easy to rationalize being right.

The emotions that bind the attackers become infinitely stronger when they attack physically. The other group will, of course, attack back in self-defense. Then they, too, bond into a tight unit.

Our "leaders" who start wars
are offering up intense emotions that imitate intimacy.

They hope to be valued for it. As physically abused children bind more tightly to abusive parents than do normal children—known as trauma bonding—*war creates connection.*

The human need to bond into community has been distorted by the need to medicate shame.

The natural, loving communion that would arise in shame-free families and a shame-free culture is a gentle bond, motivated by positive, loving feelings. It reflects who we are as humans. It is our humanness. It doesn't need to be strong because it permeates our entire being. It leads us to work well with others. It isn't a sacrifice that requires intensity for maintenance. It isn't even discipline. Discipline isn't needed. It is a forward draw that feels wonderfully good. Shame deprives us of living like this all the time. Shame deprives us of living without war.

Chapter 12
Join or Create a Shame-Healing Group

The next seven chapters describe approaches to healing shame, particularly the need to do it with others. They are only a start to addressing shame. Shame-Healing Meetings create an environment in which ways to heal become clear and possible.

We can heal our shame
and claim full life.

The most powerful step you can take to heal shame is to work with others in a group setting. It is *essential*.

I have often witnessed the difference between hearing a person tell me what she feels shameful about, and her experience of telling a group of people who are there for the same reason she is. In individual sessions I am only one person who listens intently with empathy and compassion, and who accepts her. While this is powerful for someone who hasn't been able to reveal shameful experiences, when she gives the same information to a group who listen the same way, the effect of reducing shame is magnified many times over.

Can you imagine reaching the point where you can tell a group of people something you have never been able to talk about, and see six caring, compassionate faces looking right back at you, people who carry their own shame and fear of revealing it? This is one of the powerful functions of 12-step groups based on Alcoholics Anonymous. As each member accepts the other members, that acceptance is reflected back to him or her.

In Healing Sexual Shame workshops I have watched women move from fearfully wanting to say nothing to eagerly waiting until they can talk. It is immensely comforting to grasp that others have had similar experiences and emotions.

As men come to trust other men in group therapy, they admit to behaviors they thought they would never tell anyone. The surprise is that almost every time that happens, more than one other man has the same shameful story. As men heal their shame they become capable of intimacy—sometimes for the very first time.

Options for Shame-Healing

I am presenting these options in order of value.

- Thinking about the subjects in this book may help you grasp what has happened to you, and what you want to do about it. But thinking keeps the information inside and limits the reduction of shame.

- Writing what you observe and remember and are thinking will take it outside yourself. This is more useful than thinking alone. Reading what you wrote to someone will help even more.

- The next level is finding a few friends who want to heal shame together. Three or four of you can study acculturated shaming and use this book as a guide.

- Forming or joining a group of sixteen to twenty people that meets weekly increases the effectiveness of shame reduction because these are enough people to create a subculture. As members are in agreement about the harm of shame, and study together how it appears all around us all the time, you will be in a group with those who see things that are not seen by the typical American. Adopting these views by yourself can feel isolating. Doing so with a few friends is better, but you can still feel separate. Interacting weekly with a lot of people and being able to occasionally attend even larger groups make this change in perception much easier!

Between meetings, those intent on shame reduction can meet with a few other members to study together. Go to the shame classrooms—movies and malls and restaurants and coffee shops and family gatherings—and study.

These are also the co-healers you can contact when needed. My own practice, as I have said, is calling co-healers early in the morning, leaving messages, and listening to my messages before sending. Years ago I belonged to a group of co-healers, and I asked each one how early or how late I could call. With this information, I could more comfortably enter into painful memory experience and know I had support.

- I recommend psychotherapy for optimal healing. Almost anyone will find additional value by having a therapist focus on one's personal history of deprivation and abuse. The increased personal attention can jumpstart the process. Group therapy reveals shame systems more effectively.

My colleagues and I hold Shame-Healing Groups. This is not group therapy and doesn't evolve into a "process" format, which requires therapist skills. The process format is the nature of deep psychotherapy groups that are limited to eight members. They may be all women, all men, or mixed. See www.NoShameOnYou.com for information on leader training.

Shame-Healing or Psychotherapy?

Each member of a Shame-Healing Group can discover if this format for healing shame is sufficient or if therapy is needed for extra assistance. It may be possible to attend psychotherapy for a while, and then shift to the Shame-Healing Group. Some will find that individual therapy is required before it is possible in a group to face the shame that will emerge for discharge.

Group leaders may see that some members are not able to engage in the process without more help than is allotted in this setting. He or she may then refer individuals to therapy groups. Members may also make this suggestion.

Chapter 18 explains more about how to make this decision.

Beginning Your Own Group

Having a leader trained in shame-healing groups and healing his or her own shame is advisable. This can offer the safety of someone looking out for the experience of members.

While it is better to have a leader, it is possible to begin your own group without one. This book can be used as a study guide for both led and leaderless groups. My co-healers and I are available to consult as you get started. We also have training for people who want to become group leaders. Leaders do not need to be therapists, but do need to understand shame-healing and to have been addressing their own. Classes are held in Los Angeles. A schedule is available on www. NoShameOnYou.com.

Shame-Healing Group

The initial Shame-Healing Group of about twenty begins with questions to elicit topics that might have contributed to early shame. Some examples are: What was going on with your parents when you were born? How did you experience their love as a toddler? What losses and separations did you have before age five? Did your parents' religious values convey shame? What was your earliest sign of inadequate parenting? How do you feel shame in your body? How do you avoid feeling shame?

As you can see, questions come out of the information in the book. Responses and the emotions that come with them are welcome and respected. Grief that may free one of historical shame is encouraged.

Learning the skills of shame-healing is primary.

Leaders will use a curriculum, but each group can evolve in directions appropriate to its members.

I am always in wonderment when, as each person talks, the group softens. Those who were tense and reserved melt into eagerness. Everyone feels shame, but with many pairs of non-shaming eyes, it doesn't hurt as much! Knowing that everyone else feels it when they are talking, too, brings a sense of togetherness in this project. Each one sees that the other person is not bad. Instead, they are attentive and involved. This is mirrored back as they see that they are a member of this community. If no one else is bad, then you aren't either.

Chapter 13

Observation

When we can see, denial lifts,
we grieve, and we change!
It's as simple as that.

I want to emphasize an overriding principle of healing shame: Observe! Learn how to see cultural shaming, self-shaming, childhood shaming, and how we are shamed every day.

Don't Make Yourself Change!

Traditionally, the culture's methods of change involve setting out to make it happen and shaming ourselves into it. This won't work. *Shaming yourself will work against stopping the shaming of yourself.* This is why I emphasize setting out to *observe, and observe only.* Trust that seeing increasingly clearly will automatically bring about emotional change.

Setting out to stop shaming will add more shame. Because social values include not failing, if you fail to change at the pace you have laid out, then you will add more shame to your internalized accumulation. This will slow down its elimination.

While having a goal of change can actually prevent change, it is possible to engage in *a practice.* This would include meeting regularly with others and setting aside study time. There is no success, or failure, at conducting a practice. There are no tests for the amount learned or skills mastered!

The solution to changing your life is all in the
practice of observing.

Observe without Shaming

As I began studying how people handle shame, I criticized them for how they avoided feelings. Over time I came to have compassion for their methods. I had to have this acceptance of others in order to examine myself.

If you shame people for how they shame, and how they avoid feeling it, you will inhibit your education. You will shame yourself, too, which will make it hard to take a look at how you also do what the other person is doing.

Observe with Compassion

It may be hard to have compassion in the beginning, as seeing people shaming each other is something the culture shames! If a parent tells a child that she is stupid, and never do that again, don't we look at each other with the expression of, "Oh my god, how could she say that to the little girl?" We don't see that we are doing to her exactly what she did to the child.

As with the entire study of shame, just *observe your desire to shame people*. Don't stop!! Just notice. How does it feel? What would it feel like if you didn't shame others? What is it like to shame with co-healers? What is it like if none of you shames? This information can help you open up to internally motivated, automatic change.

Observe Automatic Change after Shame Drops

This is pleasurable observation! While healing shame I have encountered many instances of my own that seem to have nothing to do with shame. I describe some in the Afterword. When shame is down we don't have to defend against it. You may find gossip less interesting. I discovered being able to experience a warm, loving sensation in my body when talking with co-healers and others that diminishes when memory-shame emerges for further healing.

One woman stopped being afraid to be home alone and no longer compulsively set the house alarm. Another became able to ask questions in airports or stores and felt freer to move in the world. A man found that he no longer felt dependent on his wife's approval, and was able to leave a well-paying job for one that he loved. I found that I could more easily see who, of the people I ran into, was able to relate intimately with me, and have wonderful brief exchanges. A co-healer discovered that she could just look at her husband when he shamed her, without defending herself and entering into their classic circular argument. When he got no response he eventually stopped.

I had an amazing discovery after being in the hospital with a severe infection that required surgery. I found that when preparing food, I had become strongly motivated to eat well. It wasn't from thinking about eating well; it came from loud voices in my head yelling NO! to foods that were of no use to my nutritional needs! I have long eaten a baked potato with cheese and sour cream for dinner as it takes no time. But when I started to prepare one, the No! voice screamed out that this was a waste of digestion, eat something useful! I used to make an exception to my usual diet in restaurants with excellent white bread and slather it with butter. But after the illness, the voices screamed out No! to the server who tried to put it on our table. I didn't let them scream out loud, I spoke calmly, but in my head there was no way that white flour was going on my table. Luckily, my friend didn't want any either!

This kind of change was so very easy! It didn't require reading about glycemic index, how the pancreas squirts out insulin to store the flour as fat, how the blood sugar is disrupted, which disrupts mood, how this all encourages type 2 diabetes—and from that, deciding to forgo white bread with a few exceptions. This was how I had controlled myself into health. But now my intuitive knowing has taken over, and I have no choice.

I knew this change was from more than having been sick and needing to restore nutrients I lost when not wanting to eat at all. It came from drastic shame reduction that allowed me to truly care for myself! If I value myself, and the body I live in, and the experience of having steady blood sugar in comparison to highs and lows, then I am not going to want to eat high glycemic foods. It's very simple.

Shame allows us to hurt ourselves,
whether that's as simple as diet
or as complex as addictions and depression and suicide.

My ability to observe shame with my co-healers increases steadily as we continue learning to see. Along with all other aspects of shame-healing, the ability to see—which means removing denial—increases more rapidly when done with others. We make a point of telling each other when we have seen a form of shame we hadn't recognized before. Once I could see that shame allowed me to ignore my body's nutritional needs, I told my co-healers. This helped them realize that their selections of unhealthy food were caused by shame, too! I didn't understand until my choices changed. Telling my co-healers might speed up that change for them.

A client was able to learn how to stop receiving shaming from his wife, and so he didn't revert to his usual method of *getting judgmentally angry in order to not feel shame.* He told his friends. His story made it easier for them to recognize when they received shaming and how they stopped themselves from feeling it.

Observe with Understanding

When I noticed my loud voices saying, no, don't eat that, I didn't understand that my shame had somehow dropped sufficiently so that I could truly want, from the inside out, only food high in nutrients that would keep my blood sugar steady. At first I thought having an infection that would have killed me before antibiotics were available had triggered a true desire to be as healthy as possible. As I talked about it with co-healers, it gradually became clear that it was from the reduced shame. Here's the progression. First, the healing of Avoidant Attachment allows me to receive the love of many people. Then this *evidence of being loved pushed remaining shame aside, and out came the inherent desire to eat well.* Isn't that wonderful to understand? Without co-healers I wouldn't have put this together. Without co-healers it wouldn't have been possible.

Being able to understand people who are defending against their shame offers freedom and expansion. No longer do you have to react, feel defensive, prove them wrong, or feel shame when defenses don't work. *The best defense is understanding!*

A friend and I experienced an example of the difference. A server came to our table and acted out the part of a made-up lovely person who was very interested in us. She enjoyed this presentation even while I could see she was in great emotional pain. I felt a sensation of it.

I asked my co-healer what she had observed, and when she said she didn't like the server, I asked her to reflect on why the woman acted like this. Immediately she grasped the level of shame underlying the behavior. Then she could join me in extending a sense of compassion, an energetic acceptance and sympathy.

If I hadn't said something to my co-healer, I would still have observed. Talking, however, made the experience more valuable. It allowed us to extend love to her together. By sharing the experience, we both had a powerful understanding of why people develop false selves. By seeing clearly, we didn't feel compelled to respond to the false self. I didn't offer the expected smiles and head nodding. Instead, I could look at the server seriously, and reflect her real self back to her. I don't know if this was useful, but I do know that I was able to offer her something different from those who believe the presentation. And this is better for me.

When out in the world, observing with a couple of co-healers, you might invent what people are experiencing. Don't worry about accuracy. Look at the woman in the grocery store who is impatient with her children. Perhaps she is afraid her husband is having an affair, or they can't pay the mortgage. What shame might she be abating? How often does she speak this way to them? Your stories will become increasingly accurate as you learn how to perceive what is going on with others. A great deal of information is available as we remove the inhibitions created by shame. When we can't know about ourselves, we can't know about the stories of others. But as we claim ourselves, developing the ability to have our emotions—including shame—we can see so much more! The best education is right in front of us. We can become able to perceive what is occurring everywhere.

It is possible to continually heal shame and become able to understand the motivations of those around us. This frees us from making up why they behave as they do. Developing the ability to *observe with understanding* is powerful! It is life-changing.

Memory

Any emotional change is assisted by observing the experience of past feelings and beliefs, now false, (memory) alongside the present true ones. All of us have flashbacks—not only combat veterans—but they vary in intensity. Those physically abused will have body memory and dreams that are conditioned from earlier life. Bringing up old fears, as do combat vets, offers a chance to discover that the fear is no longer needed inasmuch as the person is no longer in combat. This realization is not an intellectual one, in the same way that the loss of someone to death isn't completed by understanding. Both require emotional grieving (see Chapter 17: Learning to Grieve).

Attachment deprivation and conclusions based on it
require an emotional process
to heal them into the past.

Dreams and emotional flashbacks are the means by which this can happen, but if not understood as productive, they are merely seen as uncomfortable, meaningless events.

By setting out to stop using some of our defenses against feeling shame, we offer freedom to these old areas that need healing. When I removed my biggest defense decades ago by deciding to not have a man in my life for at least a year, I confronted sleepwalking terrors, hearing people in the house, and feeling as if I were dead. I met with my co-healers almost every day, and grieved my way through the process. In a few weeks, I felt wonderfully alive. I have since addressed defense removal, and healing of what appeared, in smaller increments. I prefer that approach!

More recently, as I continue to combat shame, my early morning voicemails allowed me to remember that my life was full of love even while seeming devoid of it. I had *memory* and *truth* at the same time. Since only one can be accurate, grief then releases the memory, and healing is automatic.

Clearly there was nothing I could do to stop feeling as if life had no love or meaning. I couldn't decide to stop. The step I could take was an action I had committed to when I had felt full of love—talking to a co-healer. This action didn't bring about change. It allowed me to observe. This is all I have ever done to heal emotionally and spiritually. This is in contrast to physical healing, which assists shame-healing, too. For that I went to doctors, learned what would help me feel my best, and did it. This included treatments, supplements, diet changes, and a lot of reading. It would be so nice to use this regimen with shame-healing! Take nine supplements and exercise five days a week! (Sherry A. Rogers' books offer a great education on achieving complete physical health.)

Chapter 14
Study the Culture

Once you have established a group—close friends, a Shame-Healing Group or a psychotherapy group—next is *observing*, as I described in the previous chapter. *Ordinary, everyday shaming is the most difficult to observe because it is integrated into the culture and seems normal.* It's a special study because we have to be able to see how we are all shamed every day in order to stop receiving it.

If you print up the list of shame examples from Chapter 6, Ordinary, Everyday Shaming, and have it in front of you, this kind of shaming may seem more obvious. Recovery programs and psychotherapists have lists of emotions for people who have difficulty recognizing what they are feeling. They can look them over and select one. You can use a list of how people shame for the same purpose.

Television and magazines are, as I mentioned, a source of examples of lots of shaming. Sitting with co-healers, pause DVD's or DVR's and discuss the shaming you observed. If you disagree with each other, play it back and look again. Acculturated denial may make it difficult to see when shaming is right in front of you. Take your time. Remember my example of shaming the hospital nutritionist in front of audiences, and not one realized I was shaming her even when I said that I was giving an example of shaming.

You can create a practice of studying how people abuse each other, how everyone shames everyone, and how people spend much time in the victim triangle. One approach is to *assume all communications and facial expressions are shaming, and then search for those that aren't!* Go to a coffee shop, sit with a drink, and watch. Notice how those taking orders are feeling. What do they hide from customers, and what do they reveal? What are they gossiping about when the store closes? How much shaming is in response to the person it is directed at, and how much is a response to everyone all the time? Is the person aware that they are putting others down, or is it habit, or rationalized?

Imagine how you would feel if you were the person you are observing. What if you were the husband with the wife impatiently tapping her foot? The person behind the Starbucks counter who asks how the customer is and gets no response? Or gets a flat Fine, thanks? How would it feel to be the mother of the child who loudly complains that he now wants a drink after the order has come? How would it feel to be that child when the mother shames him? Why has he asked for something he knows won't be given? What would you feel as one of the people you observe fighting in a restaurant with quiet voices and very serious faces? Can you imagine being the bank teller who told my client that he should have known which account to make his deposit in? What might she have been responding to? Perhaps he was playing victim, and she responded with abuser?

Watching teens is informative because they shame each other and themselves in ways that are transparent. Perhaps this is because they belong to a different sub-culture, and so it is easier for adults to notice their shaming behaviors than with people in our own sub-culture. Or it may be the immaturity of their age that makes them stand out. Their shaming is very obvious to me because I am not around teens very much. Those of you who are may have lost sensitivity to their everyday interactions.

Instead of shaming teens for their criticisms, put them in your classroom. Observe.

My colleague with step-children tries to control the TV programs they watch and proclaims the harm of shows that rely almost entirely on shaming. Perhaps they do portray stereotyped ways of interacting, but adult shows do this too. *Frasier* was based on lying and shaming, which included self-shaming. *The Daily Show* with Jon Stewart is a good source for a new look at news, but is based largely on shaming typical media coverage. The humor of *Everyone Loves Raymond* was built around the main character's response to shaming, which was seen as deserved. Even shows not dependent on shaming still include a great deal of it.

Study each of your environments one at a time. Begin with the least triggering, such as stores you frequent and places where you don't interact with people you know. As you approach the store, remind yourself of your task. Be prepared to study facial expressions and body language of the other shoppers and those working there. Listen to voices and sounds and tones. See if you can prove that someone isn't shaming rather than that they are! If you feel confused over whether or not someone is shaming, talk with a co-healer. Take someone with you and talk about it right there.

Notice people acting as if they feel shame. This may be a signal that they have been shamed. Were they? They may believe they are because of deeply internalized shame. Are they reacting to a particular person, or do they always seem to feel shamed?

Observing without Language

If you have a chance to go to a country with a different language, hanging out in public places and listening is a great way to grasp how shaming goes on in all cultures and appears the same (allowing for cultural variations). With co-healers, make up what people are saying. Without words to inform you, your information will come from body language, tone, facial expression, movements, and a general sense of energy. People who are shaming or feel shamed will have a hardened sense about them. They will seem to be pulled back—or pushed forward. There is no soft, flowing, smiling ease about them.

Chapter 15
Study Your Personal Experience of Shame

First, what is your *physical experience?* Is it in your stomach? Skin? Throat? Do you hold your breath, taking in as little air as possible? Take a moment and check in right now. Let yourself relax, and notice all areas of your body. Then think of something that makes you feel bad about yourself. How did your body change?

Tell co-healers so you can see it more clearly. This awareness is needed to assist healing shame. Being able to observe it helps you know what you are healing.

Next, study the *emotional experience.* This sensation can be more difficult to perceive because it is the very one you also want to avoid. The physical sensation is easier to recognize as separate from the emotional pain. Breathing deliberately can support awareness. Call to mind something that will bring shame, but this time study your reaction. As you recognize physical sensations, does it change the emotional ones? How can you describe the pain? Do thoughts tend to follow? See if you can interrupt the thoughts in order to allow the emotion to flow. Read below about breathing to assist you in staying with the emotion. *To heal shame we have to feel it, let it move around in us, and breathe it out.*

Know that you can stop this exercise at any time. When you have had enough, use any of your methods of stopping it. If you do this with co-healers—always the best approach—then turn to them with a comment or joke, anything to distract you from the shame. *Knowing you can stop makes it easier to keep going.*

I had a non-shame experience of this after a tooth extraction that left my jaw frozen. When my surgeon forced it open a little, I experienced a slight panic as I had no control over the pain. When I did it myself, I could easily tolerate mild pain because *I had control over it.*

Anytime we subject ourselves to pain, it will be easier if we truly know we can stop at any time. You have lots of time. Feeling it in small increments is effective.

It can be difficult to see that being depressed, waking up feeling dead, wanting to rage without knowing why, desperately wanting a drink or a drug, feeling lonely and isolated, and a long list of other symptoms are actually caused by internalized shame. Shame can be felt directly for what it is, or it can be distorted by what we use to fend it off. The need for avoidance can be so intense that the shame itself isn't felt.

Each of us can discover how we avoid shame, and then inhibit the method for a moment or an hour or a day to see what happens. Use Chapter 8: Overriding the Experience of Shame, to create your own list of ways you use to avoid shame. Put anything that is common for you on the list even if you aren't sure that you use it to avoid shame. You can determine its function later. Then, whenever you find yourself acting on one, check back to moments before that and see if any shame might have been trying to surface. Our favored methods are very effective, and it takes some study to discover how they work.

Next you can set out to deliberately stop using one of your methods. Only one, as you don't want to invite all your shame to appear at once. This would be too much pain. The study at this point is just becoming aware of your methods of avoiding shame, and what it feels like if you don't.

I have long since healed shame I'd felt when eating in restaurants by myself. But if I hadn't, I could deliberately go to a restaurant, sit down, order and eat, all the while watching my shame come up. I could watch for the sentences associated with shame. These might be something like, "What's wrong with you?" "Don't have any friends?" "What are you, a loner? Some kind of alien with no one of your kind here?" "No one likes you, huh?" "Well, obviously something is wrong with you. No one chooses to eat alone, do they?"

I might have answered these voices by affirming that, Yes I am alone, but just because I like to be alone doesn't mean there is something wrong with me. I would have watched how shame moved around in my body, and invited it to flow. I would separate this physical sensation from the emotional one, the one that pulls me down, makes me feel small, and urges me desperately to do something, anything, that will make this go away. I would ask where those voices originated. What was I still believing that made me feel shame when being alone? What is shameful about being alone?

This would be easier when I set out deliberately to tackle this life inhibitor. My shame would already be reduced because I would know that it isn't deserved and can be healed. When I didn't know that, then all I had was the critical voices and head-shaking over how pathetic I was.

Breathing deliberately encourages the shame to flow around in you and out. Practicing yoga or Pilates can take you into your body, and breathing becomes automatic with practice. Choose the Yoga asana that allows you to drop most fully into your self. For those with Pilates experience, a simple roll-up will automatically engage breathing. Perhaps continue until you have to breathe deeply and grunt to keep going, imagining the shame being pushed out.

You may want to try something new, but using methods that your body already does automatically will take out one more step in telling yourself what to do. Run a short distance, walk uphill, chop wood or do anything else to quickly increase breathing.

We inhibit breathing when we don't want to experience emotions that have made it through other barriers. If you attend to your breathing when feeling any kind of distress, you can invite it to move instead of stagnate. We can actually tolerate horrible feelings if we can discharge them.

Body workers have methods of grounding their clients to prevent that free-floating sensation that can come after body work, or when avoiding what is going on with their emotions. You may be able to ground yourself by walking. In a personal growth seminar we were told to find a warm place with dirt to walk in with bare feet. Use anything that gives the sensation of your feel planted solidly on the ground. When shame begins to mount, see if it helps to focus attention on your feet.

Many writers have addressed methods to bring oneself into the present. Mindfulness is a term for this. Learning how to engage the present reality serves to counterbalance the historical experiences that emerge and are now invited to be healed. Many of us have learned that *the loving, safe present alternates with the terrifying, painful past in the service of healing*. Shame is the foremost emotion that belongs in the past, and to keep it there, we must let it flow out of us by engaging our knowing of the wonderful present.

Some writers indicate that learning to stay in the present is an end in itself. Life will feel better. Yes, and healing old shaming will allow it to feel even better still! I briefly went to a therapist who used mindfulness techniques to feel good. But she was riddled with patterns of behavior prescribed by the culture and her own past that prevented her from relating intimately with me.

Twenty years ago a client gave me a quote from *Transformations*, by Karlfried Graf von Durkheim, in which he talked about how meditation can be used to confront each new demon in order to heal it. He said not to use meditation to feel good and peaceful, but rather to obtain the truth—to *heal* those demons. Many will be satisfied to just avoid demons and have a life like that therapist.

Rules for Shame Study

There aren't any! If you notice that you are beginning to create rules about how to observe, and what to do when you see shaming, it could be because rules add order and make sense of things. Wanting rules, or creating them, is a way to manage discomfort. It's a way to manage shame. And of course you can do it, anyway.

If others create rules and want you to follow them, the above still applies. Rules are merely ways to create order when there actually isn't any. They offer a sense of meaning and purpose and predictability that doesn't exist.

Of course you can use them if it makes this process easier. There are no rules about not using rules, either! We get to use any and all of our defenses against shame until we don't need them any longer.

I have observed people creating a rule that one's spouse must stop shaming. This is usually applied with shaming, such as, "You're shaming me! You're not supposed to do that!"

Chapter 16
How Do You Shame Yourself?

Internalized shame becomes such a part of our identity that all people shame themselves in the ways they were shamed. Some are obvious, such as saying, "I don't know why I do that," "What's wrong with me, I can't do anything right." Another example is comparing oneself negatively to others. A friend enjoyed watching when I had my home remodeled, but expressed her admiration by comparing herself to me. I knew her reflection of my knowledge and ability was genuine, but it was offset by the comparison with which she put herself down. I wondered what childhood relationship seemed to require letting someone else win when there was actually no competition.

One victim stance is having it bad while others have it better. "How did they do that? We worked hard but they have it made. What's wrong with us?"

Self-shaming is required by the culture. "I'm sorry I didn't sweep the floor." "I'm so stupid." "Now why did I do that?" "What was I thinking?" "I'm a failure." "I'm so sorry."

Self-shaming can appear as
depression and anxiety.

These symptoms may arise when people believe they are so unacceptable that belonging isn't possible. Anxiety can come from fear that shameful qualities will be found out. Panic attacks might arise from fear that traumas occurring in childhood will occur now, but also come from the horror of feeling the shame that accompanied them.

Believing that you don't deserve anything, that you aren't entitled to love or a nice life, is shame. Humanness brings with it the right to belong in a community and develop ourselves to the fullest. No one is on the outside. Shame can interfere with knowing this. The person who feels unworthy (shame) will feel not entitled to belong. People who buy what they can't afford, or gamble compulsively, or shop addictively, or focus on wanting what they can't have are suffering from shame that prevents them from understanding that we all truly deserve belonging.

Self-Shaming to Avoid Shaming Others

I have observed clients, friends and co-healers change the subject from how they were harmed to how they harm. Some parents can't discuss how their mothers treated them because of feeling guilty for doing the same things. Self-shaming can actually feel less painful than taking a look at other horrors that need to be faced.

Shaming to Motivate Oneself

I mentioned the young man at the pool who actually got out, stood on the side, and berated an imaginary person in the water.

Internalized Shame Is Hard to See

I have given examples of shaming directed at the self that can be seen, once the role of the culture is clear. However, all internalized shame is actually a form of self-shaming. Once it is taken in and believed, it is directed at oneself. This can be hard to recognize because of the myriad ways we prevent ourselves from feeling shame.

If I tell my friend that she is working too much and taking care of everyone else's needs to avoid feeling internalized shame, she can look at me as if I'm a little crazy, and say that her job and family just require so much. It takes exploration to challenge the defense against shame and allow the truth to emerge. Once the shame about being good enough drops, then she gets to understand the right way for her to spend time, and do it. But that means challenging the supporting beliefs that she is good for working hard, and she is good for raising a family and taking care of extended family members.

Earlier I mentioned the internalized shame reflected in my alien status that prevented me from enjoying being alone. I didn't realize that not being alone in restaurants was a defense against that shame. In looking back I recognize that I had great shame from using Avoidant Attachment as a lifestyle.

Chapter 17
Learning to Grieve

*The ability to grieve
is at the top of the list of
skills needed to heal shame.*

The anger and sadness that comprise grief are the emotions that allow us to change our perception of life from what it once was to what it is now. When someone dies, that need is obvious. It is just as necessary when grieving past trauma and deprivation, so that we can see the beauty of life.

It is said that time heals, and of course time passing does make a difference. However, when grief doesn't discharge hurt and shame, they remain in place as if they are still somewhat occurring. This can be seen in "unrequited love," where the person who is left remains strongly bonded to the lost one. While this is romanticized as true love, it is actually lack of grief. It may be from ineffective grief where sadness is felt but isn't accompanied by necessary anger.

Since our society inhibits healthy anger and healthy crying, the resulting deprivation of the ability to grieve has left all of us with shame from childhood. If we had those emotions intact, we would have grieved it all out a long time ago. *Now we can re-learn to use those tools for leaving the past in the past in order to have a full present life.*

Grief has been a subject of Attachment Theory researchers. The first of John Bowlby's trilogy was called, *Attachment*; the second, *Separation: Anxiety and Anger*; and the third, *Loss: Sadness and Depression*. The titles convey the experience of grief. First, there must be an attachment to a person, or a belief, or a way of life. Loss of any of these brings anger and sadness.

Babies angrily cry when their mother separates from them. The objective is to get her attention so she will come back. A baby's instincts tell him that if Mother doesn't return, he will die because he would have, centuries ago in the hunting and gathering days. This anger is natural to all of us when we lose something we are attached to, as our primitive brain isn't dominated by the cerebral cortex which "knows" that the person has died—or left, or the house burned down, the belief proved wrong, and so on.

When we are grasping that the loss is complete, then sadness and healthy depression arrive. We are accustomed to the experience of losing someone to death by shedding tears and turning inward—a working depression. This helps alter reality, from including that person to not including him. The more unexpected and tragic the loss, the stronger the crying and depression.

Anger and tearful letting-go alternate until resolution is complete. After that, occasional sadness comes up over time.

These emotions that release things and people important to us are the same that allow us to heal from hurts. When children fall down and skin knees they run to an adult and cry. When they are done, they get up and run off. But over time our culture teaches children that when they are hurt, not crying is better, and anger is not a good emotion. As a result, *the very tools that allow us to be hurt and then grieve it away are impeded.* It is possible to experience horrible atrocities and then rage and cry until the effects are cleaned out of us. We *can* leave the past in the past. First we must reclaim the right to have the emotions to do so.

Shame cannot be healed
if the emotions of anger and sadness
are not available.

Meeting with groups can help those who cannot grieve easily to access these old emotions. The shame of crying, especially for men, can ease by watching others cry with no shame. When the absurdity of holding back tears is seen for what it is, shame can dissolve. Anger can be better understood in groups, too. As members learn what real anger is, and how the ways it was expressed toward them as children weren't healthy, they can become more comfortable letting it roll out of them. Accessing emotions is a vital step in the process of finding complete recovery.

Physical Health Brings Productive Grief

The American Psychological Association published two books in 2004 establishing that past trauma can cause physical illnesses of almost all kinds. My experience and that of many clients has been that undergoing health practices allows grief to flow more easily, and shame-healing to speed up. These practices include: detoxification, healthy diet, giving up smoking and alcohol and harmful foods, exercise and other healing approaches. We have experienced that trauma healing is faster when alternative health methods are used. It is likely that feeling better from these approaches will make it easier to tolerate discharge of shame and fear.

I highly recommend the health books of Sherry A. Rogers, M. D., which cover all areas of alternative health. They are available on www. Amazon.com.

When Emotions Are Not Grief

Tears to Override Anger

People who aren't comfortable being angry may use tears to change anger into an emotion that feels safe. For example, a client was talking about how horribly his father had treated him with beatings and criticism of everything he did. When I said, You're angry with him, he nodded and started crying. I told him to stop the tears and let himself have the needed anger. He was then able to tell me how when he was eighteen, he had finally punched his father to stop him from hitting his mother. He saw that I enjoyed hearing about the anger that had finally created a boundary. Then he could release the shame he felt for hitting a parent!

Anger to Override Tears

Other people are comfortable with anger, but tears are frightening. Another male client cannot tolerate any evidence that his wife isn't interested in him when she doesn't pay what he considers sufficient attention. He projects deep sadness from having been the child of a mother who paid no attention, but he learned to use anger to avoid the pain. Stopping him as I did with the other man was ineffective. I learned that if I let him be angry, and gently reach out to the hurt child several times, he would eventually tolerate some of the sadness.

Grieving for Loss

The emotions that arise when someone dies are probably the most familiar kind of grief, because they are socially acceptable. It isn't well understood that this is an opportunity to grieve for other losses where such strong emotions aren't permitted. Any time emotions of grief appear, it can be helpful to ask if they seem to be for more than the circumstances. Let them come, even if people look at you strangely because your expression is over the top! Take advantage of the opportunity.

When beginning physical detoxification, I found that emotional detoxification came, too. I discovered reruns of a sitcom that engendered regular tears because the mother was so sweetly loving to the children. Since I was grieving deprivation in my childhood, I TIVO'd every episode and watched them all twice over a matter of weeks.

More recently I took my beloved cat to the vet because he had blood in his urine. Two days of antibiotics didn't help, so I took him back, only to learn that his newly diagnosed hyperthyroidism had caused weight loss and high blood pressure, which caused his retinas to detach! The vet wanted to keep him for the day to feed and hydrate him.

When the assistant came to take him from me, I started crying. I cried all the way to the parking lot, on the drive home, and the whole rest of the day.

A small portion of the tears was for my cat's poor health and his fear of staying at the vet's, but I knew most were for enormous losses in childhood. I talked with my co-healers, but didn't learn what actual loss I was grieving. I didn't care. This grief was painful because it included losing someone or something. I still welcomed it, knowing what it was doing for me.

I always welcome tears!

Grieving for Abuse

Anger and tears for abuse feel different in the body, and may include body memories. Our bodies retain memory of what happened, and the sensation can emerge along with grief. I once had pain in the muscle in my upper arm that felt as if something had hit it. When I rubbed it, it hurt. I could still play racquetball, and it was gone in two days. These are both indicators that it was memory, not a real injury.

This kind of grief is enjoyable because it is easy to grasp that old hurts are being cleaned out. However, if the abuses were too intense, and if shame came with them, the psychological defense mechanism of dissociation may appear. People can find themselves unable to think well, wandering around the house or stores, wondering what they were doing. This is a time to call a co-healer in order to remember the present, and know that this is a good thing even if it feels very strange.

Grieving Out Shame

This seems to be the most difficult grief of all. It means feeling the shame. So while tears and anger are doing their job, it still feels terrible to feel shame. It's necessary, though. I find that the grief feels good, but the accompanying cloudy, icky sensation that comes with it doesn't. Call a co-healer to get help identifying what kind of grief you are having, and get support in letting it continue until it lets up. Ask to be reminded that when it is over, you will get to discover what you healed! And that new freedoms have come.

One Friday I was having a wonderful day at home and in my office, seeing a few clients, writing, talking with close friends. I felt fully alive, in my life, and needing nothing more. When my last client left

I was aware that I felt bad, cut off from everyone, and with no life. I looked back over the day and could see the contrast, which allowed me to suspect that memory emotions were coming up to be healed. When they emerge it is often hard to remember that they are not real life. After a half hour, I realized I had to call a co-healer. I left a message with the details, and she called me back. I was so in the memory of being unlovable and unloved, and the Avoidant Attachment that accompanies that belief, that I didn't know my friend loved me and was there for me. I couldn't sense her presence, I only heard her words from a distance. It was like having a relationship, but at that moment, not believing it.

I talked about the subjects that had come up in my session, searching for a clue as to what had been triggered: my client's abuse, the shame he carried, the pain inflicted along with constant criticism by his father. This man carried tremendous shame from his past and from what he had done in his adult life. I felt deep compassion for his struggles. And somehow, in spite of his intense shame, he was able to hear me. He recognized that I don't shame him and am here to help. He is making significant changes because of it.

I made some guesses about my own history, but nothing was clear. I watched my emotions for the rest of the evening, finally going to bed, my question unresolved.

The next morning I left voicemails for another co-healer. By the time I was listening to my second message, I was crying! It was grief at having my love received. A few days before, I had asked her if she needed to talk, after hearing that her voice sounded stressed in a voicemail. I told her I was here for her. When she called back, she was touched, and welcomed my caring. My love was received! Somehow that triggered the pain of deprivation of such an experience when I was a child. Then the session with a man who was also condemned and deprived touched my unhealed pain. This pain could emerge to be grieved away now because after releasing so much shame, I deeply know that I am loving and my love is received. Thus I could cry *only* for childhood. There is no adult corresponding situation. *Shame-healing allowed this old experience to arise for healing, too!*

Then my awareness of my friend as a deeply loved person in my life returned. The detached, disconnected feeling was only memory of living that way in childhood.

This crying emerged without my understanding, and I welcomed it anyway, knowing that it would release more of the deprivation of childhood love and attachment—and that accompanying shame. It felt really good because I wasn't crying for a loss, I was crying for a wonderful gain!

The following morning, I woke happy and alive to a rich day before me. It was rich not because of planned activities, but because in this present-day life all my days are rich.

Unhealthy Grief

Some crying can actually reinforce shame. This happens when the person is berating himself. This kind of crying doesn't yield a sense of release after it passes. The grief seems to be remorse or confession, accompanied by a sense that nothing can be done about it. It is difficult to perceive that shame is just history that needs to be grieved away.

When mental health professionals assess depression, they ask about tearfulness. Some crying is a symptom of depression. It is necessary to differentiate healthy, freeing grief from stagnant, clinical depression. For the latter, supplements and occasionally anti-depressants are called for.

Chapter 18
When It's Time for Therapy

Shame-healing groups have been designed for people who know there is something more to life but haven't been able to figure out what it is. They may have gone to therapy or marriage counselors but find something still missing. Others haven't felt the need for therapy or antidepressants but still aren't satisfied with how life has unfolded. Learning how the culture shames everyone, and seeing how it has affected their lives, can bring satisfying change as you get to stop obeying inappropriate rules and discover what life could be like.

Others have struggled with depression, anxiety, addictions, and other ways of trying to handle the layers of shaming incorporated over the years. Some who have been exploring reasons for their distress will find shame group to be just what they need. This includes those who have gone to marriage counselors or therapists and been helped.

Still others will find their emotional symptoms too intense to be handled in a leaderless group or one led by someone who isn't a psychotherapist.

I have named a few of the reasons for selecting psychotherapy instead of shame-healing groups. *If these groups are not fully serving the purpose of healing shame in a comfortable, curious manner, more help is needed.*

Many people will be able to heal shame by gathering together in No Shame on You, or informal, groups. Others' shame will be too great to be able to address this painful emotion without more comprehensive assistance. If shame is too high to see other people clearly, or anxiety or depression is too strong, a therapist can help.

Those who had secure attachments, and received less family shaming than usual, are, as I said earlier, able to more quickly learn to see shaming, stop taking it in, and stop doing it. The rest of us have to go through a more difficult process. Therapy can help explore the whole picture, including abuses and poor relationships.

Toxic shame is perhaps the worst emotion we feel. We get to admit this, and know that when it is intense we need help. Individual therapy and group therapy together offer the most powerful experience. Individual therapy addresses traumatic history that brought shame. The relationship with the therapist becomes a source for grieving out the deprived relationships of childhood.

In group therapy members learn about their typical ways of using shame, and how that shows up in relating with others. The breadth of understanding, and the tools for healing, are far deeper than in shame-healing groups. This may provide more rapid and deeper healing.

Those of us who grow up with abuse and abusive relationships project both onto people and situations in the present as if they were still occurring. When this happens in a therapy group, it can be identified and assisted and healed. The therapist and group can help members understand why they feel as they do, and how to grieve it away. But when such projections happen in No Shame on You groups, the leader and members don't have the skills to handle it. A person could feel shamed by the group's reaction, which is not conducive to healing. This is the time for the group's leader or members to suggest that a therapy group would better serve the person's needs.

Strong anxiety or fear—reactions to childhood trauma—may indicate a need for therapy. Fear of people and situations is miserable, and of course prevents seeing who the other person really is or what is really going on. It made sense during the trauma, but no more. Since strong fear makes other people uncomfortable, individual, as opposed to group, therapy may be best in the beginning. A psychodynamic therapist understands the need to be the object of the fear and anger. Clients need to project all their past ways of relating onto the therapist whose job it is to receive them and use them for the healing process. Grieving out the memory and the accompanying resulting shame offers freedom to live without fear.

Some Ways to Assess the Need for Therapy

- If you believe that you need assistance, or just want it, then it's the right choice. Since therapy is more helpful in healing shame, then merely wanting to use that approach is the basis for a good decision. The combination of individual and group offers a powerful assault on this dreadful feeling and healing from attachment deprivation, trauma, and other causes of internalized toxic shame.

- Some people will find that their experience of being shamed is so strong that they can't believe that group members aren't shaming them. In this case, being in a group with a therapist will assist with learning how to heal from an individual history of shaming.

- Others have difficulty seeing how they are shaming and may engender conflict without understanding why. Therapy groups are equipped to help with this.

- Those who need to handle their own shame by perceiving their difficulties as someone else's fault will need a therapist to address the intense emotions that come with letting this maneuver go.

- Others find it hard to give up their belief that their difficulties are all their own fault. This will interfere with shame-healing in a non-therapy group and is better addressed by a therapist.

- When members find themselves angry and argumentative with the leader or group members, it can be a result of the classic manner of avoiding shame—defensiveness. During a talk I gave a woman argued intensely with me when I suggested that saying "I'm sorry" can very often be a shame medicator and not really needed. She told me forcefully that it would be rude, and how could I think that way. Her therapist has been questioning her very slowly to help her learn about the causes of her shame. When the need to medicate shame is so high, the best route is discussing it at a pace one can tolerate. Shame-healing groups will not be served by arguing, or by slowing down to accommodate someone like her. And she will not obtain the benefit she is after.

- Leaders and group members may assess a member's need for therapy. If an individual's shame is too intrusive, and it creates a disturbance for the group as well as the individual, then a referral is in order. Healing shame is a challenging process, and groups need to run as fluidly as possible for the benefit of all.

Finding a Therapist

Psychotherapists and counselors have a wide range of styles, approaches and skills. Many are focused on symptom relief and finding solutions. Others attend to belief systems, knowing that if beliefs change, emotions will change too. Some spiritual counselors assist people in feeling better through engaging in spiritual practices. While research has demonstrated that all these approaches are helpful, they don't address comprehensive healing of shame.

When HMO's came into existence, short-term therapy was covered, and so therapists studied how to get as much benefit in as few sessions as possible. This served those who couldn't afford to pay what insurance didn't cover. While clients may feel better after six to twenty sessions, deep underlying shame and cultural shaming aren't approached. There isn't time.

The approaches that address the fullest healing of humanity are the ones most likely to assist with deep shame-healing. Foremost is psychodynamic therapy, including the New Psychoanalysis. Highly trained therapists study all the projections onto present people and situations from past trauma and depriving and abusive relationships. Therapists conducting Trauma Therapy may also offer a long-term, deep look into history.

When selecting someone, ask how they view shame and what role it plays in their work. Indicate that you wish to heal shame that began with a depriving attachment and then compounded by effects of the culture. If he or she doesn't respond with interest, the therapist may not be a good fit for this purpose.

Chapter 19
Thoughts, Observations, and Experiences while Writing

This chapter comes from experiences I had as I wrote this book, healed shame and worked with co-healers to safely stop avoidantly attaching. It was interesting to look back and see what I was struggling with. When I started this project I thought that no one had enough time in life to heal all their past traumas, the effects of the culture, and all the shame we carry. Now I know that I can do it. My pod of co-healers can do it. We have the skills and the dedication, and we have created the connection that will serve us in accomplishing this amazing undertaking.

False Communication, Rules and Intimacy

Culture-wide shame has resulted in the evolution of false relating among people. When we lose access to our spiritual nature—our community nature—we must invent rules to replace intuitive knowing. I have studied these rules and practices for a long time and am learning how to stop engaging in them.

When someone asks me how I am, for example, when required to by their employers, most of the time I don't answer. The person required to ask doesn't seem to notice or just doesn't respond. But occasionally someone does react. A woman who was checking me into a hotel apparently was invested in getting an answer. When I didn't say anything, she stood there across the counter staring at me. She asked a second time. When again I didn't answer, she continued to stare, waiting. Then she repeated the "How are you" with her teeth clenched. It was obvious that I wasn't going to get my room key if I didn't do something, so I said, "Fine," in a dramatic way. I hoped to communicate that I was merely responding to her question out of obedience, not because I really meant the answer.

I was thrown by her intense desire for a response and her anger, and so I wasn't able to think about how I would have liked to handle this situation. I could have said, "I'm a stranger to you, I can't believe that you really want to know how I am. Aren't you asking because you were instructed to as part of your job?" Then I might have found out that she feels insulted when people don't answer, and I could talk about how I really can't give a real answer in this brief exchange. We could have discussed alternatives for her to say when people don't answer. Some of my friends have learned that I don't ask how they are unless there is something significant in their lives. Those who ask how I am will receive their real reply, and then go on to say, "Well, I'm doing well, too," and give me information. They know that I don't follow the prescription where each asks the other and listens to the response. They do know that I am interested, and that I do want to know even if I'm not asking.

Travelers wanting to engage usually begin by asking where you are from. This kind of rote question is necessary because most people have been cut off from their intuitive knowing. When meeting someone new, we don't know what might be of interest to both.

I am practicing talking about something other than the question of where I'm from, or asking a question of my own. I could say, "I find it interesting that you begin talking with strangers. Do you do that a lot?" I could find out if they use travel as a time during which they make casual friends, if they like to do things with others, or if they just want to talk to someone other than their spouse.

The argument in the back of my mind says, Oh, just give the answer! It's no big deal, it takes seconds, and they will feel good. But I know it isn't right for me to do this. *I have to heal from operating within the shameful culture.*

Shame Solutions Become Cultural Values!

Enjoying Being Alone

As an Avoidant Attacher, I have always enjoyed being by myself. However, because I was a dependent child, the use of this defense included my being in the physical presence of adults but with no inter-action with them. Thus, going to restaurants, Starbucks and grocery stores brought a comfortable sense of safety and belonging. People are all around, but I don't have to talk to anyone.

I used to deprive myself of this pleasure because I believed that those around me saw me as strange. When I became old enough to go to restaurants by myself, and then to travel alone, I was uncomfort-able because I feared that others would think I was incapable of making friends or having a husband who wanted to be with me—as if the right choice was to be with others.

I didn't notice this shame until I began flying by myself. I discov-ered that I loved long layovers. In an airport no one expected people to be with others! I could fit in and belong even while acting out my Avoidant Attachment.

As I wrote this, sitting alone at Starbucks, I watched a very obese young woman with exceptionally large buttocks place her order. When she sat to wait for it, she had to pull the chair way out from the table to make room. What must that be like? She cannot avoid shaming looks and comments. Most obese people believe that being thin will remove their shame and life will be good. It doesn't work for long. Only one kind of shame will be eliminated.

Shameful Behaviors

A woman at Sports Authority showed me mouth guards. She said the one she uses to prevent grinding her teeth at night is best because it helps with drooling, then "admitted" that she drools, in a tone that invited me to smile with her to offset the shame. Why feel shame over bodily functions?

One morning I was still in my bathrobe, after breakfast and be-fore bathing and dressing. A man I didn't expect came to my door to do some work my contractor had ordered. I had to walk out to my gate to show him the problem. I was aware from the moment he knocked that I wasn't supposed to be in my bathrobe, but, out of character, I felt very little shame. My shame-healing is going well.

Why do we have rules about when you should bathe and dress? I think it's something like, you aren't doing anything useful or productive if not dressed. Or, you aren't living your life. In fact, I was living my life as fully as if I were dressed. I have to determine this for myself and not judge based what others think. I imagined that he assumed I just sit around watching TV all day.

I see some of my remaining sources of shame showing up here. I think I am worthy of not being shamed if I work, if I don't waste time, if I don't watch TV during the day.

I noticed a whiny, victim-like tone when I told my racquetball partner that I hadn't gone to the challenge court for a Friday evening event of all men while she was away. Once I noticed and checked in with my feelings, I saw that I was operating on the idea that if I were a truly committed player, I would have gone and taken my turn to play. I couldn't just acknowledge that I wasn't comfortable going without her and being the only woman/mediocre player. The men are friendly, nicely tolerant of us, and ratchet down their games to play with us.

Solutions for Healing

In mental health and recovery communities, reasons why a person is shame-based are examined. I have pursued this study for my own reasons, even writing a book called *Treating Sexual Shame*. I learned to recognize when I was being shamed, and how I shame others so I could have boundaries and stop shaming. I am getting quite good at both.

To give up methods of avoiding feeling toxic shame,
I have to recognize
the ways we all avoid feeling it.

I motioned the person to go at the four-way stop at the same time he motioned me to do the same. We smiled, and I went. I took pleasure in this generosity. When I drove on, I realized that we both got to feel like good people, and we both got to receive appreciation from the other for being good. We felt connected. Perhaps this was a genuine caring for each other and wanting to make things go smoothly. It may also have been a method to avoid shame by feeling good about ourselves.

My confidence in my intuition grows the more I strip off denial of how extensive shame avoidance is. It can feel genuinely good when someone does something for me, yet other times it is clear that the person is only trying to get affirmation. Before I trusted my intuition, a gas station attendant in cold Alaska offered to check the pressure in my tires just as I was about to do it. As soon as he began, I knew that I was supposed to walk around the car, appreciating each tire. Instead, I got in my car to stay warm—the only reason to accept his offer. Driving off, I wished I had done it myself so that I would have lived the truth. I had let him do it because I didn't want to seem rude, saying no to a kind gesture. But as Bradshaw says, being kind is actually hateful. It set the attendant up to hate me for not responding as I was supposed to. It set me up to look ungrateful if I said no—and if I said yes.

I had to be strong to tolerate knowing how shame-resistance prevents people from really connecting. I had to feel strong while living alone with far less interaction with others than I had ever had. This prepared me to realize how alone we all are most of the time. This is the truth. And, it is this truth that will allow us to live in the present, in reality. We all want to fit in and belong.

If we follow the rules for medicating everyone's shame,
we truly don't fit in and can't belong
in any connected way.

Walking through several malls, I found myself looking at the people. I used to believe that most of those around me were happy and had satisfying lives. Even when I began practicing as a psychologist, I thought my clients—and I—were the ones with problems, unlike "normal" people. Somehow I thought it was better to believe that I could be like the happy ones if only I completed some magical process.

That lie sustained me. Perhaps in childhood it truly did sustain me. I lived in fantasy, imagining the adult life I could have as soon as I was old enough to create it. These fantasies were conscious. Only now am I coming to recognize the fantasy of believing that people around me have comfortable, loving, meaningful lives with only occasional external stress. I thought that anger and shaming and other harmful behaviors were either appropriate, or the person exhibiting them was crazy. It has taken until now to allow myself to grasp the truth that *every single one of us was harmed in childhood*. And that all of us struggle with our choices about how to handle internalized toxic shame.

This makes me angry. As I walked among the people in the malls, I raged inside over the isolation each one is living. This raging pulled off another layer of denial, letting me see this tragedy more clearly. I have more raging, and more denial-pulling-off to do. It has been incredibly difficult to see how alone everyone is. I had to know this before I could create a pod of people who will say everything they feel—naming when they are operating in projection from the past, or from fear or shame. They are people whose intuition is well enough developed so they can know when they and I are telling the truth, people who are willing to name anything going on even if it triggers that dreadful experience of shame.

Here is the amazing benefit of knowing how separate people are. Nothing other people do is surprising. Never again comes the question, Why did he do that? If the behavior seems irrational, or unexpected, or dramatic, or even crazy, I will know that this person has discovered this way to avoid feeling as if he or she isn't worth being alive. Or, his methods don't work and he feels the horror of very old shame.

A man was disliked by his neighbors because he was an angry, vengeful person. After a few months of my speaking to him in a friendly way, he became angry when I built a small building on my property, reported every suspected infraction to the county, came on my property to inspect it, and damaged things in small ways. He lied to my workers about things I had done. The construction foreman was upset, and wanted to triangulate with me against this bad person. I didn't join him. I didn't believe this man would do anything truly destructive, he was causing trouble in the name of righteousness. He has truly horrible ways of avoiding his shame. This is exacerbated by the effects of alcohol on his liver. The methods he uses to avoid shame harm his physiology, too.

Being Hated

When my client glares at me hatefully I know it's because I have looked him in the eyes and said I know he is lying. *He hates me instead of feeling shame.*

When another client angrily told me she wasn't coming back, I knew that her shame had been triggered, too—the shame of truly not wanting to change. Instead, she wanted support to stay in her old patterns.

In the past I tried to get myself to operate in some manner that would make the other person feel better and not think I was harmful. This was stressful because it failed most of the time. I could never figure out exactly what the person needed.

I have the freedom, now, to flow through life, seeing. It's not stressful when I can stand back watching someone work hard to avoid feeling shame. *A vital outcome of seeing is that I don't have to shame others!* Or is it the other way around—because I don't have to shame them, then I can see?

It must be both. As I heal my own shame, I don't have to shame others in order to medicate my shame. And, as I am more present to the truth, I can see more clearly that they don't deserve shaming and criticism. Criticizing others shamingly even in my head was such a barrier to being in the present. If I'm making things up I can't be in the present.

It's more powerful to be angry when necessary, and to firmly point out the truth when someone is doing something harmful. But that is all there is to it.

While I am becoming freer, others can be uncomfortable with the truth even delivered in a non-shaming manner. A friend began drinking heavily after a life trauma, and recognized that she is an alcoholic when she had difficulty stopping. I pointed out that her teenage son was harmed by her addictive drinking. This was too painful to bear. I believe that if I had shamed her for it, it would have been less painful because her long practiced defenses would have leaped into gear and held off the shame.

Winning

I have recently healed from unconsciously directed failure to win at competitive games. When playing racquetball with someone at my level, I used to lose more than win. If I got ahead I would suddenly not be able to play well. Isn't this odd in a culture that believes that winning is better than losing?

If you lose, then you have to be a good sport about it. In other words, *you can't express the shame and upset over not meeting the requirement to be shame-free and happy.*

If you don't win, the next value is doing your best. Then you are acceptable. Why do your best? Isn't enjoying yourself good enough? In fact, if we were shame-free, enjoying ourselves would be the primary reward, and because we are social creatures, it would include enjoying ourselves with others!

I couldn't control this need to lose, but eventually the healing process allowed me to play my best all the time! Suddenly I beat my partner every game by a lot. I watched my emotions as the games progressed, while I continued to win point after point. I felt separate. I was alone. I was isolated.

I haven't yet learned the reasons for this isolation, but healing shame of all kinds allowed me to even claim being visible when winning, too. I became comfortable for the first time while being watched as I played. It made no difference at all.

Shame down, life up!

When I received my Ph. D., I opened a nice office, had supportive colleagues, a new car, new professional clothes, a lovely home, and a family. I wore a very old watch with the gold plating chipping off. I didn't want a new watch. I clung to the physical evidence that everything in life wasn't perfect. I hadn't entirely won. As if this was going to make me safe from what the losers would do to me if they perceived me as winning.

Limited Intimacy

We do have intimacy, of course. While living in Hawaii, I had a circumscribed experience of it. I frequently visited a beach that was rearranged by a river several times each winter, then sand would be replaced by the ocean. I loved monitoring the rapid geological changes. One day I was walking along the wild river marveling at its effects when a man passed me, smiled, and said, "Incredible, isn't it?" I said, "Yes!" We had a perfect moment of shared pleasure. Intimacy.

People in combat share real intimacy because it is necessary for survival. They need to see each other's real needs and meet them in a communing, team-work manner. *Human instincts motivate us to meet real needs*, one's own and those of others.

I sometimes cry in front of my TV over the lack of intimacy all around me. When watching these characters having powerful experiences that require their entire humanity, I grieve for the lack of it. As my denial pulls loose, I can see why these shows feel good. Now, instead of joining in a false life with the characters, I grieve for the very need to have these scenes! I appreciate how good writing and acting can take us into these very feelings that we are designed to have. We get the satisfaction of using our humanness. How tragic that we want to experience this through lives portrayed on a cold screen!

Following politics beyond obtaining information and deciding what to do creates another way for people to engage in what feels like human community. In real life, being ER doctors and nurses, 9-1-1 dispatchers, EMT's in ambulances, and firefighters are career choices that allow people occupied by the very immediate needs of others to disengage their shame for a time. This feels good to those who live with shame.

Offering Intimacy Everywhere

I so appreciate my automatic commitment to healing—my Feet— as they got me to study shame, and then become different. I had already known that my Avoidant Attachment needed examination in order to release it. Looking at the pervasiveness of shame all around us, being able to accept people as they are, insisting on living with truth, and seeing that I had accepted my mother's shaming by the very process of proving her wrong, moved me to grasp how I can offer myself anywhere. I mustn't wait around until I find people who are capable of intimacy! What an absurd approach to finding humanness! (I am not shaming myself. Absurdity is real. It doesn't imply shame-worthy.)

Living the Truth

Shame gets us to lie, to deceive, and to withhold information to avoid being shamed by others. It prevents the intimacy that requires revealing ourselves.

> *If we heal shame*
> *we will automatically tell the truth.*

Deceiving causes us to feel shame. It supports the very shame we are trying to medicate with deception. So one approach to healing shame is to learn how we are deceiving, then experiment with stopping.

We create boundaries against being shamed. Without full access to our humanness, we have difficulty knowing what good boundaries are—which ones are really needed. On the phone, my client tells his father that he has to meet with a customer when the truth is that he is bored hearing the same stories over and over. He can't tell his father that he heard the story before, and could they talk about something of interest to both of them. This would be a self-caring, non-shaming solution.

If the father reacted predictably, and shamed my client for these comments, the son could let the father know that he isn't to criticize anymore. Period. Then wait to see what happens next. The father may want to hang up, or shame some more, or apologize. My client doesn't know, because he has never set boundaries to find out. I do know from years of working with clients that the father will change. Not an internal, healing change, but a behavioral one. He will grasp that *the system has changed.* His son has changed. He will have to act differently in order to have a continuing relationship. This is all my client needs—to have his boundaries respected.

The first task when telling the truth is *knowing what the truth is.* Dishonesty is more than obvious lies or secrets. I have practiced perceiving what is going on with others for years, and naming both that and what is going on inside of me. But of course this is only practical with close friends who agree that they want this kind of revelation, and with clients who pay me to tell them. Sad to say, hearing my observations can bring shame even while I am truly not shaming. The very needed awareness and communication provoke shame associations from the past and from the culture. We all want intimacy, but being seen is frightening because we fear our badness will be seen too. Of course, it is. If it weren't for the dreadful experience of shame, we would want to know how we are harmful so we can change!

For a long time I assumed that I couldn't tell the whole truth to strangers or acquaintances. But now I see that *if I hold myself back, I make myself alone.* So I am venturing out to see what to do when the grocery clerk asks me how I am and I know he really doesn't care.

After decades of learning how not to lie, I came to see that I have to give up every bit of lying, including saying, Fine. The very day I was pondering what to do, instead, I played racquetball on a court that I was to use only when with a person who lived in the complex. Our court was being refinished and my partner and I didn't want to stop playing for two weeks. We couldn't find other options that didn't include becoming members of a club. My friend who lived in the complex unlocked the door of the court for us two times, but the third he was out of town. We went anyway, hoping a court had been left open. It hadn't.

When I asked a member if he would open the door he looked at me strangely, explaining that the key to the outside door would do it. Now here is where in the distant past I might have wanted to say my friend was late and he had the key. Even when I didn't lie, I always felt a little shame about doing something wrong, and wanting somehow to make the person think I wasn't. But this time I told the whole, absolute truth. I didn't look down or away. I said that we didn't live here, and my friend who did isn't here to open the door. Done. My energy flowed forward toward this person.

The man responded with the desire to meet a real need, which had been presented in an honest, real way. He had no interest in judging me for using the court without my friend present.

I loved the open, fluid feeling this brought. It seemed like the best reward for refusing to distort things, for being fully committed to telling the truth. I didn't do it for *him*. I did it so that I got to stay with myself, alive. Racquetball went well, too, as that open, fluid, bright experience of life continued. I played really well. My partner did, too. Perhaps she picked up on my energy.

Two men on the other court did the opposite. I asked them if they could open the door for us, and they explained that they didn't have a key, that their friend had unlocked the door, left, and was coming back, but they weren't sure when. I asked about how long, and they said twenty minutes. I said I would wait. Later I realized that they were lying! The friend wasn't coming back. In fact, he didn't return. How must they have felt at the thought of my sitting in the hall waiting for their friend! Luckily, I went on to find someone in the workout room for the key. This is like the plot of so many sitcoms where lies create all kinds of difficulties.

One racquetball afternoon I was feeling low, almost depressed, and playing didn't bring me out of it, as it usually did. My partner didn't seem herself either, and I wondered if she had picked up on my mood. So I stopped to tell her about it. She said she wondered if I were reacting to her series of bad shots! Her next thought was wondering if it were her outfit. We laughed together over the automatic assessment of someone's mood as being caused by oneself, and the shame that is so tightly interwoven! I felt better after telling her.

I wouldn't have been lying or deceiving or even withholding a truth if I hadn't said anything. But it was really clear that relating in a shame-ridden culture requires revealing ourselves to those who can understand, accept, and join us in humanness.

I tell the truth as soon as I know what it is. The hard part is knowing what it is.

Being Well-Adjusted

Well-adjusted doesn't mean mentally healthy or living in integrity. Well-adjusted people have developed a functional use of defense mechanisms that allow them to basically enjoy their lives. *They have adjusted to the cultural shaming and resulting lying.* Those who *don't want to adjust* struggle with *not fitting in and not belonging.* They may struggle when they do fit in and belong, too, as that often feels self-violating.

Fear of Healing from Shame

Self-help books, including my own, promise that we will like the changes offered. While I think that we are happier when we give up old shame and our defenses against it, and live as if old relationships were still true,

> *it is truly difficult and awkward,*
> *even frightening,*
> *to give up shame.*

Toxic shame is the underpinning of the culture. It is the basis of our identity. It is the foundation of most of our choices for how to spend time and how to relate with one another. Even pleasant, productive and caring behaviors can be designed to avoid feeling shame!

Change Is Frightening

I am often asked why people change so slowly once they understand why they feel bad. Some forms of psychotherapy address the client's beliefs, because when they change, the resulting unpleasant emotions, including shame, change, too. For example, if a woman believes that she is defective for failing a college class, the therapist can help her change her belief about the meaning of failing, which will change her resulting emotions—she can stop feeling defective. But these approaches don't address the deeply held traumas and the shame that has been placed on us by history and culture. *When we change our very shame-*

based identity, we need a great experience of grief. And when the grief has had its effect, then operating in new ways requires an adjustment.

As my fear of being evil dissolved, I consistently woke feeling alive and ready for the day. As each piece fell, going out in public was more and more interesting. But after a few days of this, I noticed that I was feeling afraid! All this change was unfamiliar.

Fear of change shows up other ways, too. Fear can be about the very same things that bring no fear when I am feeling solid and safe. I can find myself sitting in my living room with a vague sense of danger, but with nothing to attribute it to. I might make up what it's about, but quickly realize that that isn't it. There are no solutions to this emotion. *It helps to know that it is either fear of change, or it is fear that I grew up with.* Then I know that it is part of a process, and it will pass when I have discharged it sufficiently. The pod calls *the fear of change, Integration Fear, and the fear from the past, Memory Fear.*

Facing fear of change is part of change.

Right along with shame and fear of shame and fear of anything else, the emotion needs space for its discharge. I let the sensation in my chest flow and I consciously breathed.

I find it helpful to think about my identity, my ways of viewing myself and the world, and my Avoidant Attachment, as *life-saving.* While they didn't actually save my life, they did make me feel safe from dying. Something that I have done for a very long time—while believing it was saving my life—would be very frightening to stop! So of course I will feel terror along with the old shame, intermixed with the new grief to let the past go.

This state of *fear* and *shame* and *grief* all flowing together needs to be tolerated in order to complete the grief and leave the past in the past. All of this is tolerable because I have co-healers.

Lisa understood that when she took care of her baby granddaughter, she would feel bad the next day. The baby is happy and full of life in contrast to the misery Lisa felt with a mother who didn't want her and hid her pregnancy until giving birth. The contrast brings this information up for Lisa to experience, which is painful. She no longer needs the life-saving defenses of self-shaming and doubting what she knows.

Sticks and Stones

Why is it humiliating when your partner has sex with someone else? Naturally it would feel bad, be angering, frightening, threatening of the security of the relationship. Communing would be lost. But humiliation? That comes from a feeling of shame engendered when seeing the relationship as meaning something about each person's worth and value. These are shame-laden ideas.

Self-esteem is one of those terms that is supposed to be the opposite of shame. It means that you feel good about yourself. *If we were all shame-free we wouldn't have a term like self-esteem in our vocabulary.* Esteem is sought in order to offset shame. It is not a genuine result of healing shame. Self-esteem is on the opposite end of the measuring stick from self-condemnation. Both are self judgments of our worth.

Bodily Shame

My son was disgusted by the idea that I put essential oils on Q tips and put them in my nose for twenty minutes to heal a chronic infection. If there were no cultural shaming, wouldn't he think it looked really funny? His sons would think that. They haven't had adult training in disgust yet.

I have been doing coffee enemas for years to detoxify my body and help my liver do a better job of this important task. Coffee enemas are a popular alternative healing practice for cancer, and for those of us who want to stay healthy as long as possible—yet no one talks about it because of shame regarding bowel movements.

Recognition of Shame

Giving up the idea that there are mentally healthy people in the world and those who aren't makes room to understand that every man, woman and child is carrying shame, differing only in degree. And every one of us is medicating it. The amount of shame can be seen on a continuum from just cultural to being deeply felt in every cell of the being. The medication of that shame is also on a continuum. On the far end are those who are in such deep pain that they resort to deadly addictions. If addictions don't work to dampen the pain, then deep depression takes over.

I have a friend who forgives people when they do things he finds objectionable. He gave the example of a driver cutting him off. As he found himself getting angry, he cut it short by forgiving the driver. This is effective for him in that he doesn't have to continue feeling angry. However, if he chose to heal his shame he wouldn't find himself raging or criticizing drivers.

Hatred can be tolerated when one is shame-free.

When I still had the shame wad deep in me, I didn't like being around people who hated me. Years ago I went into a two-week depression when a client coldly condemned me in front of group members. My reactions went way beyond those to criticism, because if someone criticized I could defend myself, showing that they were wrong. If someone hated me, especially if they didn't tell me why, I would become disorganized and not be able to think clearly. I had to end a relationship with a client who hated me and couldn't process it. I would attempt to engage her caring side, but knew that hatred was waiting in the wings.

This disorganized thinking—which is the defense of dissociation—was projected from childhood where my mother's hatred threatened my life more than once. In order to avoid her hatred, I learned all the rules and followed them. I didn't believe that the rules were right, but I did believe that I had better observe them for safety. So when someone hates me in a withheld, sort of kindly, manner, I react in the same life-preserving way I learned in childhood.

With my shame reduced, I can understand that someone's hating me is only a maneuver to avoid feeling terrible. That's okay. It's not about me.

Returning to Defenses against Shame

I would like to offer self-help promises that everything will be just fine if you follow these instructions. When I wrote about sexuality, magazines requested that I list a series of to-do steps. There are no steps. Dreadful feelings are woven into increasing love and freedom from shame and freedom to move easily in the world.

Those of us who use Avoidant Attachment as a defense feel isolated and alone, cut off from others. When asked if I feel lonely, I always say no. The sense of isolation goes way beyond lonely. *It's being so isolated that lonely isn't even possible.* Loneliness is the experience of missing those you like to be around, or needing people so much that talking even with strangers relieves it. When engaged in Avoidant Attachment, I yearn for something human, some permanent presence of others. But it can't be just anyone. Friendships won't fulfill this historic-based need.

When I am "gone," as we call it, I have little awareness of the world around me. I don't see sunshine and color, I don't smile and drink in the beauty of the red leaves on the poinsettia I saved from the year before, or the bright yellow flowers contrasting with green lawn and foliage. I am occupied by a physical sensation that might be called anxiety except that it isn't like the kind that comes with real situations. It's an old, deadened sensation. I have little experience of life, even while preparing a meal or feeding the cats. I am not motivated to do anything, carrying out only rote tasks. I am grateful that I rarely return to that deep isolation.

Samples of Ordinary Shame

We take for granted that others will feel embarrassed, meaning shameful, when doing something against the rules. Standing in line at the drugstore I overheard a very old woman in front of me say to the clerk, "My husband would kill me if I paid too much." The clerk, trying to be kind, said, "I don't think your husband would kill you." The customer said, "He can't because he is already dead." She was senile. The clerk apologized! After the woman left, the clerk said to me that she should think before she speaks!

As the observer, I can see that the clerk has absolutely nothing to apologize for. If I were in her place, I might have discomfort. We have been trained to. A person who uses defensiveness as a shame medicator might say, Hey, you said he would kill you which means he's alive! I couldn't have known he was dead!

As a student of shame, I could see that the customer hadn't intended to cause shame or defensiveness. I made up that she had repeated that line for decades. She is keeping her husband alive with her sayings. But when the clerk referred to her husband, she knew that he was dead. Her brain isn't working well enough to apologize to the clerk.

On that same trip to the drugstore, which is right next to a large retirement community, I saw a woman singing to herself. When I walked toward her, she stopped and apologized. I smiled at her. I could have asked why she said she was sorry. I could have said, No need. I didn't because it was clear that it wouldn't release her from shame. It wouldn't even free her from the immediate experience of shame. Her shame and her methods of suspending it are so habitual that nothing would be different if I just smiled. Which I did.

Communing Together to Heal

When healing from emerging forms of shame, I find it necessary to talk with people I commune with in order to lift the shame and return to communing. I know that I have to hang out in the shame, too. If I tried to get out of it when it appeared, I wouldn't be giving it time to come forward and reveal what needs to heal.

One day when I was playing racquetball at my very best, and winning every game, I noticed feelings of the dread of death. It wasn't as strong as it used to be. I let the feelings come and just observed. I was supported by the intellectual understanding that they were temporary.

Elizabeth called one late afternoon when I was walking on the beach on a warm January day. In a few minutes we could see that we were communing. She was with me on the beach in the warmth and fresh ocean breeze, though her home had been torn apart after flooding. Even while she was frustrated by her situation, and I was adoring mine, we engaged energetically. She could take in my experience. We both felt wonderful. *This is the life that is possible all the time.*

I knew that I was supposed to follow a rule that I can't be in this perfect place and fully enjoying it, if she wasn't there too. The rules are even more complex than that. I can be there, but there has to be something wrong. For example, I have to leave too soon, sigh, or the waves are too noisy to hear well, something like that. Or I could enjoy the beach while pretending I was somewhere she wouldn't mind knowing about.

I named these patterns as they showed up. They are losing their power as my shame drops. I have found over time that a pattern will first appear as a thought accompanied by strong emotion. Over time the emotion lessens until finally I hear the thought with no emotion. Finally there is no thought.

We talked about how it is necessary to expect days of up and down. The down is essential to heal the past and make life even better. I don't like this, but I understand it. I am willing, and my Feet tell me this is the path. Better to know that we are going to go up and down so we can tolerate it more easily. I have never known anyone, client or friend, who didn't go to the down place during healing. I warn people about it when they have reached a new high. I don't want them to think that the high wasn't real.

It also helps me to know that giving up old ways of being is going to bring a strong emotional reaction. We developed methods to avoid shame and annihilation and abandonment, so when we stop using them, we are bound to fear that these very experiences are impending. This can be quite dramatically challenging. After going through it enough times, *I now associate an intense negative reaction with positive change.* So instead of feeling badly for having it, and worrying about its significance, I value its significance! Is that reverse psychology??

Avoidant Attachment is shaming of others. I am judging others as not worthy of my relating. I believe others are evaluating me in the same manner. As my shame drops, I am becoming able to open my hand to everyone. If a hand reaches back, wonderful. If it doesn't, I am safe with my boundaries.

Avoidant Attachment breeds fear of shame. I am entirely responsible for myself, can't ask for help, and can't have it. This is because I am alone. I imagine that people with poor social skills have Avoidant Attachment style. We didn't learn them while growing up. I developed some when in college, but before that I was outside, quietly listening.

When I think about what *not relating* would do to a person's sense of safety in community, I realize why avoidant attachers need to be self-sufficient. If natural relating is communing with others in a mutual need-meeting way, then we would of course feel shame for our failure to do that and terror from not having the safety it brings. Our primitive minds that work this out can't let us know when communing is possible and when it's not. Shame has to be out of the way to understand. So *I am healing shame in order to heal Avoidant Attachment in order to have as much love and communing as possible!*

A man sitting next to me in Starbucks asked about the battery life of my computer. I told him. He asked how old my computer was. I told him. Then his body language communicated that he wanted to end the conversation. He must find people wanting to use him for conversation and projected that onto me.

As a *recovering avoidant attacher,* I am learning about all the ways people will interact with me now that I am open to everyone. While I have been enjoying bits and pieces with strangers, I am also learning *how little communing there is.* My healing alternates between joyfully seeing how much I've been missing and sadly grieving for the absence of intimacy.

Is it perhaps true that secure attachment would bring more internalized family requirements and cultural rules that make people feel shame? And would Avoidant Attachment only include the shame made up about oneself? Would the typical Avoidant Attacher believe he or she had some basic evil that accounts for receiving so much abuse and neglect?

A pigeon walked by and I appreciated its iridescent feathers and beautiful, complex patterning. Yet these birds are shamed for moving in, procreating in great numbers, and pooping on everything. They are shamed, based on what humans want. Other birds by the lake near the ocean are seen as wonderful and interesting. They don't bother us. I find them interesting, but I have to sneak up on them, using binoculars to get a good look. The beautiful pigeon brings himself right here to me!

Stopping Some Stimuli

Ongoing stimulation, like having the radio and television on all the time, distract from what would emerge. Setting aside times with no distractions in order to see what shows up might reveal emotions that would appear if not avoided. Giving up phoning, texting, e-mailing. Doing nothing but sitting in the yard, going to the beach. Drinking only water, nothing with alcohol, caffeine, or other mood changers. See what happens.

My Feet led me to this understanding. Decades ago I always had the radio on when driving and music or television playing at home. One day I stopped wanting the stimulation. Now I can see that Feet wanted me to pay attention to myself. Sometimes I will listen to NPR as I'm driving. I notice that sometimes I turn it on when I am tired of feeling what I am feeling! It can be interesting to notice how my unpleasant emotion might still be there, but when I have something else to pay attention to, I don't find it as unpleasant. It has taken Feet's commitment to healing to get me to stop distracting myself.

Shame-Free Curiosity

Going out in public with my computer in hand makes it possible to observe countless examples of shaming. If I listen with curiosity, my denial lifts. I see how ordinary situations such as sitting in a coffee shop reveal the culture's illness.

I sat near two men, one dressed in clothing intended to indicate he was wealthy. He told the other man how his tailor in San Francisco had suits he knew the man would like, he could walk in and be fitted in ten minutes, and the suits would be ready before he got on the plane back home. Then he talked about the different experiences of driving various expensive cars.

This man lives in great shame. Instead of believing that he was very successful and thus happy, I knew that being far better dressed and wealthy truly did nothing to heal his shame. It may have medicated it. But even this wasn't successful or he wouldn't have had to show this acquaintance how well he does.

A few years ago I would have criticized him for bragging. But if I did, I'd miss seeing how miserable he is under the presentation.

Another well-dressed young man sat slumped over, the clothing not able to create an impression. When two older men arrived in shirt sleeves, it was obvious that he was applying for something from them—a job or sale of a product. Shame made him miserable. It made him look very different from the two men he was with.

An hour later a man about fifty walked by me and sat in the next chair. I could feel his energy. He was desperately sucking on mine—an Anxious Attacher. I almost moved so I could concentrate on writing, but then a younger man joined him. I was not surprised when he showed false happiness and talked in a victim voice. Shame-based. I did not observe any low-shame people that day. I rarely do.

Anger in Healing

I have periods of free-floating anger while grieving. Today is one of those. Again sitting in Starbucks, writing and observing, I don't want to do either. This comes after talking with a friend and realizing that this writing project is truly what I should be doing. Other activities are not. I have to trust my Feet in this. However, now that I know this is the right way to spend time, I am pissed off about having to do it! It seemed easier when I thought I was strange to sit here writing every day. I made up that others wondered what kind of life do I have when the only people who recognize me are the baristas. Does she have a life? What a strange person!

I'm angry because I'm shame-free! First I want to give up shame. Then I'm afraid of giving it up. And when it's gone, I'm mad!

This makes intellectual sense, but on the inside it feels really really stupid!

Why do we cling to shame?

This is the question that has to do with fear of change. I have an identity based on my way of defending myself against shame. While my experience of shame isn't as strong as it is for many, I still operate within its limits. I used to have a pleasure quota. I would limit the amount of time I spent in a freely joyful, shame-free place. It had to do with maintaining the familiar methods of handling my mother's view of me as evil by shutting down and being very still. If I stop using those methods, then what?

I am coming to see why Feet are often struggling against Anti-Feet, who argue for shame. The struggle feels safe, whereas no struggle catapults me out into the world, able to take on anything, anytime.

While I was writing about my anger, a woman sat next to me and asked if I was writing a book. I've been surprised that in the two months I have sat here almost every day for two hours, no one had asked. They only comment on my Macbook Air. We had an animated conversation about what each of us does, and when she left I saw a shame-free reflection of me. I am writing a book, in Starbucks. I exist. I had clung to this as a shame-worthy scene instead of something very ordinary. At the same time, I have defended against that shame. Now that I can see that shame more clearly, I see what an absolute waste of energy that is! It's really stupid (said in a non-shaming way).

My identity includes being weird, strange, odd, and out of the norm—all synonyms! It also includes being interesting, provocative, and focused on unusual things. These views of myself have been seamless, so I didn't realize that clinging to being myself included clinging to the view of being weird and different!

Still at the Starbucks, two men are talking in what I would call a superior victim style, telling stories about people who have stupidly unfair practices. I smile. I had thought that the whole world was like that. Yet the successful businesswoman talked with me right here in public, amid ordinary people of the world, with no shaming of anyone! We plan to get together again. A cross-section of people walks through here. I get to be one of them now!

A woman just knocked a cup off the table and it broke. When the worker came to sweep it up the woman apologized in shame. The man nearest her jokingly said that cup was made by the emperor of China. Everyone laughed to help her override shame. This is a kind, acceptable method of helping someone not feel it. This has been going on forever—and will go on forever.

I wonder if all people with Avoidant Attachment would expect shaming from others. Perhaps this is the reason we avoid. People with Anxious Attachment still believe that something good could be coming and are willing to risk it. These people would perhaps learn more social skills in order to get what they can. We avoiders don't need social skills, but feel shame for not being able to fit in and belong. It is a protective defense to feel apart, even while knowing that it is a wrong way to live. Giving it up brings fear of what would have happened if I had never avoided. I would have been shamed to death. *I avoided shame by avoiding attachment.*

My mother looked at me with hatred, even when she acted caring. I always knew it was an act. Even when I was in the hospital after an appendectomy when I was thirteen years old, and she came every day. I was glad she did, because staying there for five days was really strange. She brushed my hair, which was the only way she could have physical contact with me. This seemed consistent with her attitude toward me, but many years later I saw that she was only able to hug anyone when clenching her arms to her sides. She never hugged any of us growing up. Now I can see that she was physically shamed. She passed that onto us by finding us unpleasant to touch. Of course we took this to mean that it was something about us.

By avoiding attachment I could pretend that the world was over there, and I was over here. I could compartmentalize the shaming to that distant arena. I could learn about myself over here.

After writing the above, I sobbed out loud. I cried for the fact that I hadn't been loved. I had known this intellectually for a very long time, but now I was immersed in the true knowing that I needed and deserved love, and that, instead, I was presented with a mother's face looking at me through a veil of hate and condemnation.

My Shame

I have found it difficult to name what brings me shame because when I see it, then I have to feel it. However, not seeing it as shame has prevented me from healing it.

In the past I envied people in A.A. who got to publicly say what they had done that was harmful, and heal from the shame of it. My shame isn't from what I have done.

Here goes. I feel shame for having no friends. That is, no close friends who join me in naming everything. Well, that's not true! I do have those friends. I have shame for seeing myself as having no friends. After all I have a co-healing pod. They're friends.

A friend from twenty-five years ago contacted me after I returned to Southern California, and we had a couple of interesting meetings. But when she said she wasn't interested in naming everything going on with us, I had no interest in relating with her. None.

I have avoided casual friendships because they hold no interest for me. Why? Why have I needed to limit my relating to people who will join me? Is it a grandiose belief that I have something better to do? That it is wasting my time? Getting in my way when my time needs to be spent elsewhere? Interfering with my commitment to creating a community of truth-tellers? Or did I just prefer Avoidant Attachment?

I feel shame for being seen as someone who has no friends. When my co-investor Bill asks me how my weekend was, I feel uncomfortable revealing that I haven't done anything social. I feel better in his eyes when I have something to report. It's not that I feel better, it's that I feel less alien when I am acceptable in his eyes.

I have often claimed that I am weird, and that helps for a little while. I am certainly different from the average person in my lack of social relating. When I can name that, the shame drops some. I get to claim my Avoidant Attachment. I get to claim my mental illness. I get to follow my Feet. I get to have freedom.

Afterword
Life without Shame

It seems appropriate at the end of the book to say a little about what it is like when shame heals, when it melts away. I'm to reassure you that I have it all together—I did what I described here and lo and behold, I am done with shame-healing. I'm supposed to tell you about all the clients I have helped do so, too, as proof that it is possible. And now I can tell you what life will be like if you do the same. I'm not supposed to write in a self-help book that the healing isn't done yet! So I exaggerated a little in the title of the Afterword. I don't know for sure what life without shame will be like, but *I'm discovering what happens when shame leaves*!

I'm still healing. I have really good skills, and I can see what is going on, but shame still bites me. It bites all of us pod members. I've told you a lot about what we do, what it's like to welcome healing as a natural part of being together. I'd like to enlarge my description by adding some examples.

Truly, the pod is an amazing group of healing people. And, at the same time, healing can be challenging, upsetting and distressing. In our last long weekend meeting, Elizabeth looked at me with intensity and said that I was brilliant to understand shame and attachment healing and to bring us all together to do this work. Suddenly I was in an altered state. She was in hyper-focus. Her face radiated an energy, a fullness, and I could see every cell. Within seconds I froze. I had no idea what she was talking about.

Now, isn't it strange to respond like that to being viewed in such a complete and wonderful way? To experience terror when my gifts and love are recognized?

Then I went into Avoidant Attachment, and for the next two hours I behaved badly. I told the group to leave me alone, don't talk to me. I frowned. I played out each memory feeling that showed up, knowing this would clean them out. Even though these people understand how this works, my reaction triggered reactions on their part. Then, in a couple of hours we were past it all.

Here's what makes what happened different from the old days. We all knew I had been triggered into an old memory. We all knew I would work through it. Each pod member told me what she was feeling and thinking, and we went about our time together. Then it was over and we went about our day. Lunch. The beach. Dinner.

Memory craziness is not just comfortably accepted,
it is appreciated as
the medium for healing.

We all knew it was good that I'd had this reaction because we all knew I would soon be through it, having removed another layer of Avoidant Attachment and dissolved another layer of shame!

Another time I shifted into dissociation, and asked if anyone was bored. Charlene said yes she was! I had to stare at her for a full five seconds before it registered that she had actually said I was boring. But with that information, we could all see that I had slipped into my intellect as a way to avoid emotional pain. And, yes, that isn't very interesting when compared to our vivid exchanges. No one expected me to be different, but they didn't want to listen when I wasn't truly present. I wasn't shamed by this, it was merely a truth. They weren't shaming me, they were naming what was going on.

Toward the end of our last day Elizabeth began acting as if she were uncomfortable. And then I was, too. Finally I walked around behind her to see if more information would arrive, and I realized that she was afraid of me. I said, You're afraid of me. She frowned and said that Yes, she was.

Now why would this be? Of course it had nothing to do with me. Old memory was coming up to be processed. So we processed. And she stopped being afraid.

The nature of having a committed group of four women who want to heal together, and know how, prevents the kind of shame that is triggered when people are mad at us or afraid of us. We have a trust that comes from experience and each other's commitment.

This was challenged when a co-healer was mad at me for refusing her contributions to this book. It triggered memory of her mother's criticism, and so she thought I was being mean and passive-aggressive. At first I was upset because I thought—from my own history with my grandmother who sent me back to my family—that she was leaving me because of something I did. My grandmother was my one attachment. I got to live with her for several months when I was three and my family was moving from one house to another with months between. She gave me back because that seemed like the right thing to do once they'd moved into their house.

But I worked it through, got out a lot of grief about my grandmother's "abandonment" and was able to have no shame over a friend's thinking that I was deliberately hurting her. This allowed me to tell her that I saw the depth of her shame and that I wasn't leaving. I was here to work it out. We immediately scheduled our next long weekend so we could all spend plenty of time helping her heal from her history and see me more clearly. But what an experience for me! This woman who I'd depended on to always love me and see me clearly stopped doing so—and I felt absolutely no shame! What an incredible result of healing!

Of course my co-healer soon became able to see me, and gave up her Avoidant Attachment. Her voice returned to sounding richly connected and caring. My reaction to this amazed me, too! My overall sense of me and my life didn't change. A close friend went from hating and criticizing me to loving me, and my life really didn't go from a loss to a gain. I know that she can project memory onto me again, and it won't affect me! This is a change that I didn't know was coming, but makes sense now that it is here.

I can only attribute this to healing Attachment Deprivation. I no longer need to use partners and friends as stand-ins for the mothering I didn't have. I truly don't need any one person to act in a particular way. I am full of love and able to reach out to all kinds of people. Of course the pod will continue to meet and assist each other in our healing, because that's life. People are meant to work together for the ends each wants, and we will commune with those who seek the same ends. As Elizabeth and I start out on a project to study children and shame, we have the backdrop of clinical experience and interest and ability to relate well. This brings us together.

My perception of people's energy and emotional availability has become crisp and in focus. I began to perceive clearly what was going on with everyone I encountered. The skills I developed and deliberately use in my office became automatic everywhere. I can recognize voice tones, false selves trying to convince others who they are, energy held tightly in self-defense, dark hatred projected with no words, smiles to reassure, friendliness that doesn't seem friendly. And then there is recognizing those who glow—people who don't need defenses. Their radiance can actually seem like a light around them. When they ask how you are, the words don't matter. They are really saying, How great to see your defenseless radiant energy! When I say, I'm doing great, I'm communicating a connection, a communing with this stranger.

While I had been able to recognize these differences among others—seeing who are defended and how—my own defenses still inhibited my perceptions. When my shame level took a huge drop, denial abated and I became able to view people with an unobstructed eye. Now I am free to move easily in the world, seeing what's going on with each person, and knowing how to engage—or not engage.

As shame lessens, we can recognize our gifts because we don't distort them with self-shaming and a need to prove something. We no longer have to evaluate ourselves in a grandiose manner (we're too good), or in a shame-laced manner (we're too imperfect). We can stop evaluating!

Communication with Elizabeth is far more vast than we had realized. It goes on whether we know it or not, but as shame subsides, we become able to believe the evidence of it. When we can't see our experiences for what they are then we're just confused.

The other night I had a terrible nightmare, my first in years. I woke all during the night with the horror, waiting until it was time to get up. That same night, Elizabeth had woken up with a panic attack and was dissociated all morning. Independently we'd had the thought that we were experiencing the same horror—together.

For years it's been entertaining to wonder about this kind of connection, but I had difficulty taking it seriously. However, as both of us have greatly reduced our shame—and Avoidant Attachment—we have reduced the intellectual and emotional clutter that prevents understanding such experiences. We believed that we were, indeed, having an experience together in our sleep. As I pondered aloud how we might have more insight into this kind of experience, we realized that all we need do is continue healing shame! *Reduced shame allows a greatly expanded perception of what is going on all around us.* It makes sense that as we clear out more and more of the clutter, we will come to take for granted communication and communing.

When developing
skills and talents and interests
our first focus is healing shame!

One of the fears I confronted was that I would be entirely alone while working rapidly toward this freedom. No one would do it with me, and no one would understand. This has not been borne out! On the contrary, now that I can see the truth about who is available for intimate connection and who isn't, I get to have lots of intimacy with strangers as well as with those I'm close to. I no longer expect it where it doesn't exist, and I can have a little whenever that kind of intimacy is available.

Shame causes the defense of Avoidant Attachment. Avoidant Attachment causes isolation. When both are gone, isolation isn't possible! Loneliness and feeling alone are symptoms of carried shame. They cannot possibly appear as the *result* of healing shame! With shame gone, I've become capable of having what is obtainable—which is a lot!

Another lovely outcome is the response of others. Many can't see when I am available, but a very many can! This includes my cats. When I went through a week of assimilating healing, and living free of shame, all five of my cats increased their delight with me. They didn't demand more, they just basked in what they got. They spent more time talking to me and cuddling, and I experienced their loving energy. It was reciprocal. Now imagine this with people who are able to do what cats do—perceive energy and drink up available love!

One turning point came when I was home alone for three days. I ran very few errands, didn't meet with anyone, and had just a few phone conversations. When I described this holiday weekend to a friend, I could hear judgmental voices in my head. Doing nothing but seeing one client, working in the yard, working on the book, hanging out with cats—that's no life. Yet this was the point of discovering no shame, and so *no judgment of my life*. More than that, I felt so full of love that those were the best three days! They were full and rich, and they unfolded as needed with no plan, no schedule. I knew that I had erased a huge amount of shame in order to do nothing of social importance and yet every moment I lead an entirely love-filled, full, rich life.

Starbucks has long been a pleasurable habit. Walk in, place feels good, order the standards—regular latte if need a boost, green tea latte if don't, size depends on mood.

When a co-healer visited, we went to the beach and had a nice healthy lunch. I felt the need for my latte, which I hadn't yet had that day. I knew we were near a Starbucks, because I know all of them for miles around. As we walked in, I realized that something had changed. The drink really wouldn't do anything for me. The warm liquid wouldn't take care of me, it wouldn't make me feel better. I wasn't safer because of having the drink built into the organization of my day. It had all been illusion. I turned and walked out, my friend with me. I haven't gone back to a Starbucks since, and have no interest in doing so!

Those defenses that structured my life, giving order and predictability and control, just cease when I no longer need them! I had given up all those I could observe in order to promote shame-healing, but didn't even recognize these! It is rather confusing, having thought that there was no relationship between shame and going to Starbucks! However, my Avoidant Attachment makes sense of it. When I avoid people and relationships, then I don't like to be home alone for a long time. Yet I don't necessarily want to interact with people. I want to be around people but not relate! This was what I needed as a child to be physically safe while maintaining my unique identity. Avoidant Attachment and shame are interwoven. As I no longer carried shame, then I no longer had to hold myself back in order to not take on shame. Now I am free to relate with others all the time. Intimate relating is wonderful, but *I can relate with those who aren't intimate because I am still me, just being me, wherever and whenever.* If I don't feel as if I have to make myself up because it doesn't matter if people like me or not, approve of me or not, then I am free to go anywhere! *No shame means no need for Avoidant Attachment.*

As reduced shame brought reduced Avoidant Attachment, I have opened up to profound experiences of warm, connected love. I can tell when my Avoidant Attachment is receding, because when I go out among strangers, I get lots of warm smiles! When I am defended, I only get fake ones—people who smile for their own needs, not in response to another person being openly available.

I suppose that life is far more pleasant because of having removed negative feelings. Then the positive ones are left. It is more than that, though. The good feelings aren't much stronger than they used to be, but they're more pure. Shame weaves itself into everything, including happiness and joy. I'm removing a damper. I'm able to have more of a natural way of life: spontaneous, delighted, loving, and grieving when needed, dreaming of being killed, too.

It's not over. I haven't grieved sufficiently for the loss of the attachment with my grandmother when I was three. I've cried; but without anger, I can't leave behind the shame that came from the "abandonment." I was the most powerful member of my family by some bizarre definition of me, and then later by appearing fearless inside my Avoidant Attachment. So how can I get mad about deserving something I didn't get? I know that my clients deserve to get angry, and need to. But that doesn't seem to extend to me.

If I can't get mad, then I must carry the belief that somehow I could have figured things out, I could have made things go right. Until I can let go of the Avoidant Attachment sufficiently to get mad about having had to develop it in the first place, how can I let go of the shame that came from thinking I was the one who could have made everything right?

I get mad when I truly understand communing, and how healthy families are supposed to be, and how my strength was made up! Yes, I was strong. But I was only a strong child! A clever, smart curious child who could figure things out. But only in a child's world. In the adult world, I was an immature child!

The healing isn't done yet!

Made in the USA